WEATHER AND CLIMATE

Britannica Illustrated Science Library

Encyclopædia Britannica, Inc.

Chicago ▪ London ▪ New Delhi ▪ Paris ▪ Seoul ▪ Sydney ▪ Taipei ▪ Tokyo

Britannica Illustrated Science Library

© 2008 Editorial Sol 90
All rights reserved.

Idea and Concept of This Work: Editorial Sol 90

Project Management: Fabián Cassan

Photo Credits: Corbis, ESA, Getty Images, Graphic News, NASA, National Geographic, Science Photo Library

Illustrators: Guido Arroyo, Pablo Aschei, Gustavo J. Caironi, Hernán Cañellas, Leonardo César, José Luis Corsetti, Vanina Farías, Joana Garrido, Celina Hilbert, Isidro López, Diego Martín, Jorge Martínez, Marco Menco, Ala de Mosca, Diego Mourelos, Eduardo Pérez, Javier Pérez, Ariel Piroyansky, Ariel Roldán, Marcel Socías, Néstor Taylor, Trebol Animation, Juan Venegas, Coralia Vignau, 3DN, 3DOM studio, Jorge Ivanovich, Fernando Ramallo, Constanza Vicco

Composition and Pre-press Services: Editorial Sol 90

Translation Services and Index: Publication Services, Inc.

Britannica Illustrated Science Library Staff

Editorial
Michael Levy, *Executive Editor, Core Editorial*
John Rafferty, *Associate Editor, Earth Sciences*
William L. Hosch, *Associate Editor, Mathematics and Computers*
Kara Rogers, *Associate Editor, Life Sciences*
Rob Curley, *Senior Editor, Science and Technology*
David Hayes, *Special Projects Editor*

Art and Composition
Steven N. Kapusta, *Director*
Carol A. Gaines, *Composition Supervisor*
Christine McCabe, *Senior Illustrator*

Media Acquisition
Kathy Nakamura, *Manager*

Copy Department
Sylvia Wallace, *Director*
Julian Ronning, *Supervisor*

Information Management and Retrieval
Sheila Vasich, *Information Architect*

Production Control
Marilyn L. Barton

Manufacturing
Kim Gerber, *Director*

Encyclopædia Britannica, Inc.

Jacob E. Safra, *Chairman of the Board*

Jorge Aguilar-Cauz, *President*

Michael Ross, *Senior Vice President, Corporate Development*

Dale H. Hoiberg, *Senior Vice President and Editor*

Marsha Mackenzie, *Director of Production*

International Standard Book Number (set):
978-1-59339-382-3
International Standard Book Number (volume):
978-1-59339-386-1
Britannica Illustrated Science Library:
Weather and Climate 2008

Printed in China

www.britannica.com

Weather
and Climate

Contents

Climatology

Page 6

Surface Factors

Page 18

Meteorological Phenomena

Page 36

Meteorology

Page 62

Climate Change

Page 74

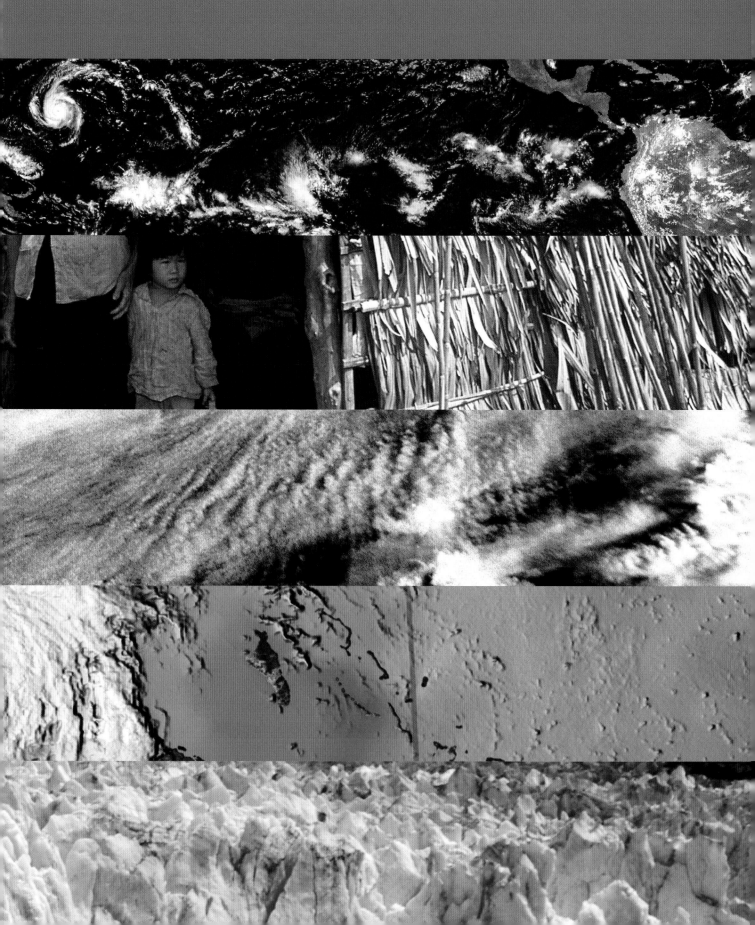

A Sum of Factors

**STRONG WINDS AND
TORRENTIAL RAINS**
Between September 20 and
September 25, 1998,
Hurricane Georges lashed the
Caribbean, leaving thousands
of people homeless.

"The flutter of a butterfly's wings in Brazil can unleash a tornado in Florida." That was the conclusion arrived at in 1972 by Edward Lorenz after dedicating himself to the study of meteorology and trying to find a way of predicting meteorological phenomena that might put the lives of people at risk. In effect, the atmosphere is a system so complicated that many scientists define it as chaotic. Any forecast can rapidly deteriorate because of the wind, the appearance of a warm front, or an unexpected storm. Thus, the difference continues to grow geometrically, and the reality of the next day is not the one that was expected but entirely different: when there should have been sunshine, there is rain; people who planned to go to the beach find they have to shut themselves up in the basement until the hurricane passes. All this uncertainty causes many people who live in areas that are besieged by hurricanes or tropical storms to live in fear of what might happen, because they feel very vulnerable to changes in weather. It is also true that natural phenomena, such as tornadoes, hurricanes, and cyclones, do not in themselves cause catastrophes. For example, a hurricane becomes a disaster and causes considerable damage, deaths, and economic losses only because it strikes a populated area or travels over farmland. Yet in society, the idea persists that natural phenomena equate to death and destruction. In fact, experience shows that we have to learn to live with these phenomena and plan ahead for what might happen when they occur. In this book, along with spectacular images, you will find useful information about the factors that determine weather and climate, and you will be able to understand why long-term forecasts are so complicated. What changes are expected if global warming continues to increase? Could the polar ice caps melt and raise sea levels? Could agricultural regions slowly become deserts? All this and much more are found in the pages of the book. We intend to arouse your curiosity about weather and climate, forces that affect everyone. ●

Climatology

The constantly moving atmosphere, the oceans, the continents, and the great masses of ice are the principal components of the environment. All these constitute what is called the climatic system; they permanently interact with one another and transport water (as liquid or vapor), electromagnetic radiation, and heat.

SATELLITE IMAGE
In this image of the Earth, one clearly sees the movement of water and air, which causes, among other things, temperature variations.

GLOBAL EQUILIBRIUM 8-9

PURE AIR 10-11

ATMOSPHERIC DYNAMICS 12-13

COLLISION 14-15

COLORS IN THE SKY 16-17

Within this complex system, one of the fundamental variables is temperature, which experiences the most change and is the most noticeable. The wind is important because it carries heat and moisture into the atmosphere. Water, with all its processes (evaporation, condensation, convection), also plays a fundamental role in Earth's climatic system. ●

Global Equilibrium

The Sun's radiation delivers a large amount of energy, which propels the Earth's extraordinary mechanism called the climatic system. The components of this complex system are the atmosphere, hydrosphere, lithosphere, cryosphere, and biosphere. All these components are constantly interacting with one another via an interchange of materials and energy. Weather and climatic phenomena of the past—as well as of the present and the future—are the combined expression of Earth's climatic system. ●

WINDS
The atmosphere is always in motion. Heat displaces masses of air, and this leads to the general circulation of the atmosphere.

Atmosphere
Part of the energy received from the Sun is captured by the atmosphere. The other part is absorbed by the Earth or reflected in the form of heat. Greenhouse gases heat up the atmosphere by slowing the release of heat to space.

Biosphere
Living beings (such as plants) influence weather and climate. They form the foundations of ecosystems, which use minerals, water, and other chemical compounds. They contribute materials to other subsystems.

PRECIPITATION
Water condensing in the atmosphere forms droplets, and gravitational action causes them to fall on different parts of the Earth's surface.

EVAPORATION
The surfaces of water bodies maintain the quantity of water vapor in the atmosphere within normal limits.

about 10%
ALBEDO OF THE TROPICAL FORESTS

HEAT

Night and day, coastal breezes exchange energy between the hydrosphere and the lithosphere.

MARINE CURRENTS

Hydrosphere
The hydrosphere is the name for all water in liquid form that is part of the climatic system. Most of the lithosphere is covered by liquid water, and some of the water even circulates through it.

3%
ALBEDO OF THE
BODIES OF WATER

SOLAR RADIATION

About 50 percent of the solar energy reaches the surface of the Earth, and some of this energy is transferred directly to different layers of the atmosphere. Much of the available solar radiation leaves the air and circulates within the other subsystems. Some of this energy escapes to outer space.

Sun

Essential for climatic activity. The subsystems absorb, exchange, and reflect energy that reaches the Earth's surface. For example, the biosphere incorporates solar energy via photosynthesis and intensifies the activity of the hydrosphere.

Cryosphere

Represents regions of the Earth covered by ice. Permafrost exists where the temperature of the soil or rocks is below zero. These regions reflect almost all the light they receive and play a role in the circulation of the ocean, regulating its temperature and salinity.

80% ALBEDO OF RECENTLY FALLEN SNOW

ALBEDO

The percentage of solar radiation reflected by the climatic subsystems.

50% THE ALBEDO OF LIGHT CLOUDS

SUN

Lithosphere

This is the uppermost solid layer of the Earth's surface. Its continual formation and destruction change the surface of the Earth and can have a large impact on weather and climate. For example, a mountain range can act as a geographic barrier to wind and moisture.

HEAT

SMOKE
Particles that escape into the atmosphere can retain their heat and act as condensation nuclei for precipitation.

HUMAN ACTIVITY

RETURN TO THE SEA

UNDERGROUND CIRCULATION
The circulation of water is produced by gravity. Water from the hydrosphere infiltrates the lithosphere and circulates therein until it reaches the large water reservoirs of lakes, rivers, and oceans.

ASHES
Volcanic eruptions bring nutrients to the climatic system where the ashes fertilize the soil. Eruptions also block the rays of the Sun and thus reduce the amount of solar radiation received by the Earth's surface. This causes cooling of the atmosphere.

GREENHOUSE EFFECT

Some gases in the atmosphere are very effective at retaining heat. The layer of air near the Earth's surface acts as a shield that establishes a range of temperatures on it, within which life can exist.

OZONE LAYER

SOLAR ENERGY

ATMOSPHERE

STRATOSPHERE TROPOSPHERE TROPOPAUSE STRATOPAUSE

Pure Air

The atmosphere is the mass of air that envelops the surface of the Earth. Its composition allows it to regulate the quantity and type of solar energy that reaches the surface of the Earth. The atmosphere, in turn, absorbs energy radiated by the crust of the Earth, the polar ice caps and the oceans, and other surfaces on the planet. Although nitrogen is its principal component, it also contains other gases, such as oxygen, carbon dioxide, ozone, and water vapor. These less abundant gases, along with microscopic particles in the air, have a great influence on the Earth's weather and climate. ●

GASES IN THE AIR

- Carbon dioxide 0.04%
- Other gases 0.03%
- Argon 0.93%
- Oxygen 21%
- Nitrogen 78%

59° F (15° C)

AVERAGE TEMPERATURE OF THE EARTH'S SURFACE

DISTANT ORBITS
Polar meteorological satellites orbit in the exosphere.

Military satellites
Air friction shortens their useful life.

EXOSPHERE
This layer, which begins at an altitude of about 310 miles (500 km), is the upper limit of the atmosphere. Here material in plasma form escapes from the Earth, because the magnetic forces acting on them are greater than those of gravity.

GREENHOUSE EFFECT
Produced by the absorption of infrared emissions by the greenhouse gases in the atmosphere. This natural phenomenon helps to keep the Earth's surface temperature stable.

THERMOSPHERE
Found between an altitude of 55 and 300 miles (90-500 km). The O_2 and the N_2 absorb ultraviolet rays and reach temperatures greater than 1,800° F (1,000° C). These temperatures keep the density of gases in this layer very low.

Auroras
Created in the upper layers of the atmosphere when the solar wind generates electrically charged particles

6%
of solar radiation is reflected by the atmosphere.

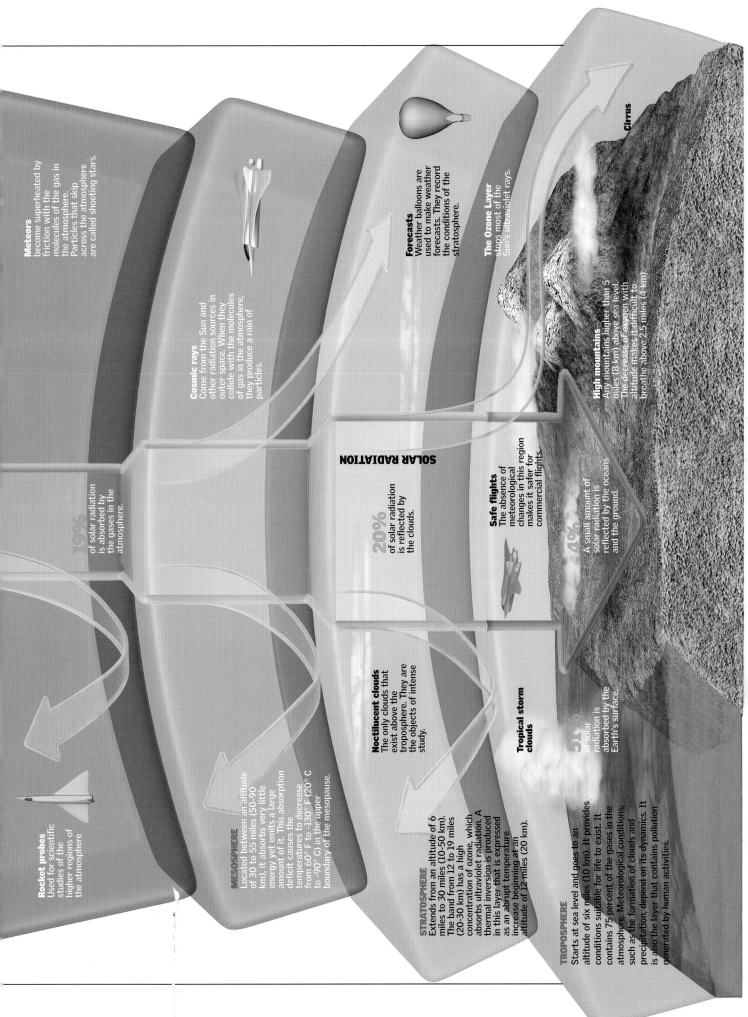

Meteors
become superheated by friction with the molecules of the gas in the atmosphere. Particles that skip across the atmosphere are called shooting stars.

Cosmic rays
Come from the Sun and other radiation sources in outer space. When they collide with the molecules of gas in the atmosphere, they produce a rain of particles.

Forecasts
Weather balloons are used to make weather forecasts. They record the conditions of the stratosphere.

The Ozone Layer
stops most of the Sun's ultraviolet rays.

Rocket probes
Used for scientific studies of the higher regions of the atmosphere

1%
of solar radiation is absorbed by the gases in the atmosphere.

SOLAR RADIATION

20%
of solar radiation is reflected by the clouds.

Safe flights
The absence of meteorological changes in this region makes it safer for commercial flights.

4%
A small amount of solar radiation is reflected by the oceans and the ground.

High mountains
Any mountains higher than 5 miles (8 km) above sea level. The decrease of oxygen with altitude makes it difficult to breathe above 2.5 miles (4 km).

Cirrus

MESOSPHERE
Located between an altitude of 30 to 55 miles (50-90 km), it absorbs very little energy yet emits a large amount of it. This absorption deficit causes the temperatures to decrease from 60° F to -130° F (20° C to -90° C) in the upper boundary of the mesopause.

Noctilucent clouds
The only clouds that exist above the troposphere. They are the objects of intense study.

Tropical storm clouds

51%
of solar radiation is absorbed by the Earth's surface.

STRATOSPHERE
Extends from an altitude of 6 miles to 30 miles (10-50 km). The band from 12 to 19 miles (20-30 km) has a high concentration of ozone, which absorbs ultraviolet radiation. A thermal inversion is produced in this layer that is expressed as an abrupt temperature increase beginning at an altitude of 12 miles (20 km).

TROPOSPHERE
Starts at sea level and goes to an altitude of six miles (10 km). It provides conditions suitable for life to exist. It contains 75 percent of the gases in the atmosphere. Meteorological conditions, such as the formation of clouds and precipitation, depend on its dynamics. It is also the layer that contains pollution generated by human activities.

Atmospheric Dynamics

The atmosphere is a dynamic system. Temperature changes and the Earth's motion are responsible for horizontal and vertical air displacement. Here the air of the atmosphere circulates between the poles and the Equator in horizontal bands within different latitudes. Moreover, the characteristics of the Earth's surface alter the path of the moving air, causing zones of differing air densities. The relations that arise among these processes influence the climatic conditions of our planet. ●

Rotation of the Earth

Equator

CORIOLIS FORCE
The Coriolis effect is an apparent deflection of the path of an object that moves within a rotating coordinate system. The Coriolis effect appears to deflect the trajectory of the winds that move over the surface of the Earth, because the Earth moves beneath the winds. This apparent deflection is to the right in the Northern Hemisphere and to the left in the Southern Hemisphere. The effect is only noticeable on a large scale because of the rotational velocity of the Earth.

FERREL CELL
A part of the air in the Hadley cells follows its course toward the poles to a latitude of 60° N and 60° S.

Intertropical Convergence Zone (ITCZ)

TRADE WINDS
These winds blow toward the Equator.

High and Low Pressure

Warm air rises and causes a low-pressure area (cyclone) to form beneath it. As the air cools and descends, it forms a high-pressure area (anticyclone). Here the air moves from an anticyclonic toward a cyclonic area as wind. The warm air, as it is displaced and forced upward, leads to the formation of clouds.

Low-pressure area

High-pressure area

Jet-stream currents

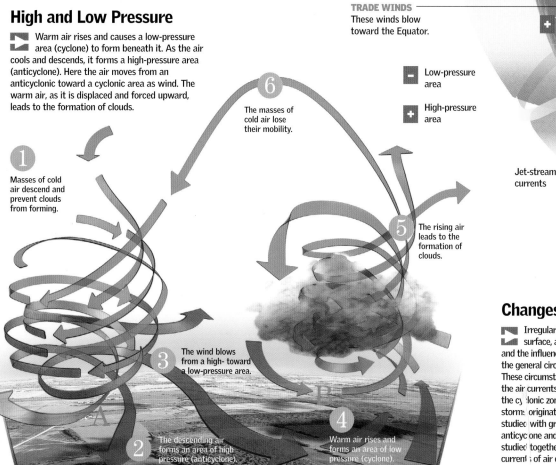

6 The masses of cold air lose their mobility.

1 Masses of cold air descend and prevent clouds from forming.

5 The rising air leads to the formation of clouds.

3 The wind blows from a high- toward a low-pressure area.

2 The descending air forms an area of high pressure (anticyclone).

4 Warm air rises and forms an area of low pressure (cyclone).

Changes in Circulation

Irregularities in the topography of the surface, abrupt changes in temperature, and the influence of ocean currents can alter the general circulation of the atmosphere. These circumstances can generate waves in the air currents that are, in general, linked to the cyclonic zones. It is in these zones that storms originate, and they are therefore studied with great interest. However, the anticyclone and the cyclone systems must be studied together because cyclones are fed by currents of air coming from anticyclones.

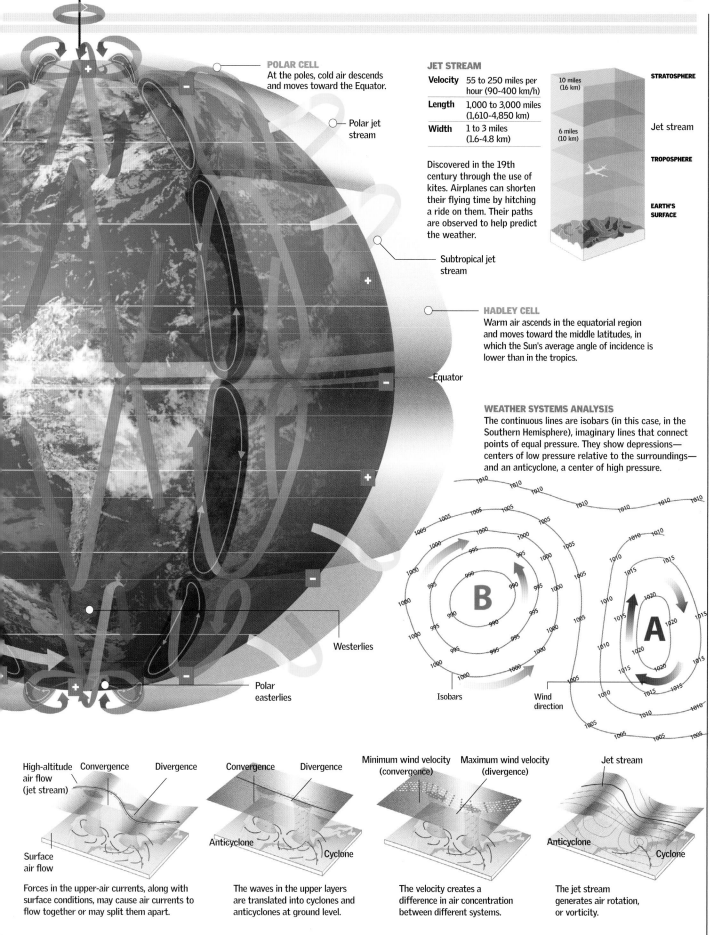

POLAR CELL
At the poles, cold air descends and moves toward the Equator.

Polar jet stream

Subtropical jet stream

JET STREAM

Velocity	55 to 250 miles per hour (90-400 km/h)
Length	1,000 to 3,000 miles (1,610-4,850 km)
Width	1 to 3 miles (1.6-4.8 km)

Discovered in the 19th century through the use of kites. Airplanes can shorten their flying time by hitching a ride on them. Their paths are observed to help predict the weather.

10 miles (16 km)

6 miles (10 km)

STRATOSPHERE

Jet stream

TROPOSPHERE

EARTH'S SURFACE

HADLEY CELL
Warm air ascends in the equatorial region and moves toward the middle latitudes, in which the Sun's average angle of incidence is lower than in the tropics.

Equator

WEATHER SYSTEMS ANALYSIS
The continuous lines are isobars (in this case, in the Southern Hemisphere), imaginary lines that connect points of equal pressure. They show depressions—centers of low pressure relative to the surroundings—and an anticyclone, a center of high pressure.

Westerlies

Polar easterlies

Isobars

Wind direction

High-altitude air flow (jet stream)

Convergence

Divergence

Surface air flow

Forces in the upper-air currents, along with surface conditions, may cause air currents to flow together or may split them apart.

Convergence

Divergence

Anticyclone

Cyclone

The waves in the upper layers are translated into cyclones and anticyclones at ground level.

Minimum wind velocity (convergence)

Maximum wind velocity (divergence)

The velocity creates a difference in air concentration between different systems.

Jet stream

Anticyclone

Cyclone

The jet stream generates air rotation, or vorticity.

Collision

When two air masses with different temperatures and moisture content collide, they cause atmospheric disturbances. When the warm air rises, its cooling causes water vapor to condense and the formation of clouds and precipitation. A mass of warm and light air is always forced upward, while the colder and heavier air acts like a wedge. This cold-air wedge undercuts the warmer air mass and forces it to rise more rapidly. This effect can cause variable, sometimes stormy, weather. ●

Cold Fronts

These fronts occur when cold air is moved by the wind and collides with warmer air. Warm air is driven upward. The water vapor contained in the air forms cumulus clouds, which are rising, dense white clouds. Cold fronts can cause the temperature to drop by 10° to 30° F (about 5°-15° C) and are characterized by violent and irregular winds. Their collision with the mass of ascending water vapor will generate rain, snow flurries, and snow. If the condensation is rapid, heavy downpours, snowstorms (during the cold months), and hail may result. In weather maps, the symbol for a cold front is a blue line of triangles indicating the direction of motion.

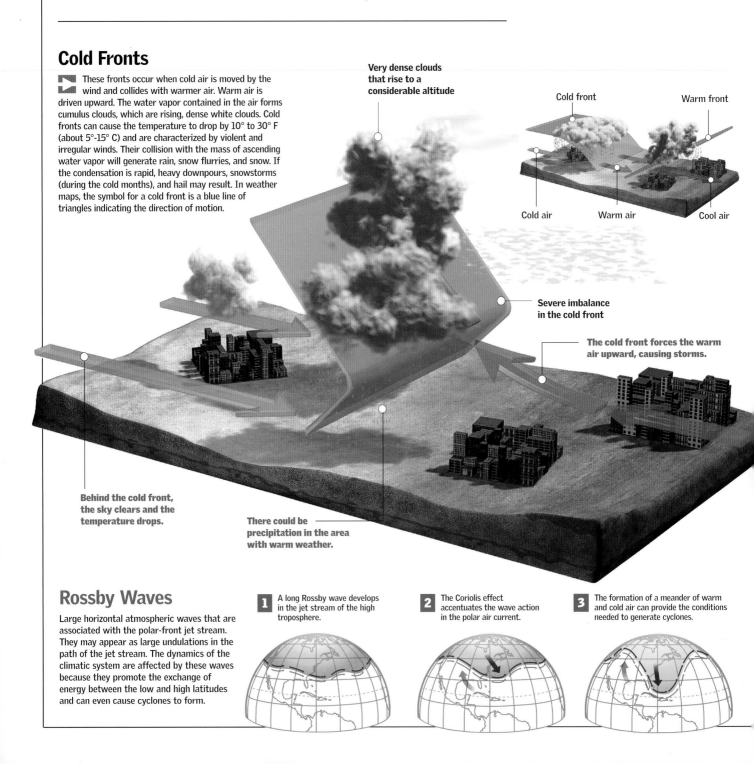

Very dense clouds that rise to a considerable altitude

Cold front

Warm front

Cold air

Warm air

Cool air

Severe imbalance in the cold front

The cold front forces the warm air upward, causing storms.

Behind the cold front, the sky clears and the temperature drops.

There could be precipitation in the area with warm weather.

Rossby Waves

Large horizontal atmospheric waves that are associated with the polar-front jet stream. They may appear as large undulations in the path of the jet stream. The dynamics of the climatic system are affected by these waves because they promote the exchange of energy between the low and high latitudes and can even cause cyclones to form.

1 A long Rossby wave develops in the jet stream of the high troposphere.

2 The Coriolis effect accentuates the wave action in the polar air current.

3 The formation of a meander of warm and cold air can provide the conditions needed to generate cyclones.

Entire Continents

Fronts stretch over large geographic areas. In this case, a cold front causes storm perturbations in western Europe. But to the east, a warm front, extending over a wide area of Poland, brings light rain. These fronts can gain or lose force as they move over the Earth's surface depending on the global pressure system.

KEY

Surface cold front   Surface warm front

STATIONARY FRONTS

These fronts occur when there is no forward motion of warm or cold air—that is, both masses of air are stationary. This type of condition can last many days and produces only altocumulus clouds. The temperature also remains stable, and there is no wind except for some flow of air parallel to the line of the front. There could be some light precipitation.

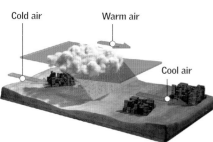

Cold air   Warm air

Cool air

OCCLUDED FRONTS

When the cold air replaces the cool air at the surface, with a warm air mass above, a cold occlusion is formed. A warm occlusion occurs when the cool air rises above the cold air. These fronts are associated with rain or snow, cumulus clouds, slight temperature fluctuations, and light winds.

125 miles (200 km)

A warm front can be 125 miles (200 km) long. A cold front usually covers about 60 miles (100 km). In both cases, the altitude is roughly 0.6 mile (1 km).

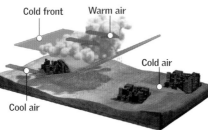

Cold front   Warm air

Cold air

Cool air

Warm Fronts

 These are formed by the action of winds. A mass of warm air occupies a place formerly occupied by a mass of cold air. The speed of the cold air mass, which is heavier, decreases at ground level by friction, through contact with the ground. The warm front ascends and slides above the cold mass. This typically causes precipitation at ground level. Light rain, snow, or sleet are typically produced, with relatively light winds. The first indications of warm fronts are cirrus clouds, some 600 miles (1,000 km) in front of the advancing low pressure center. Next, layers of stratified clouds, such as the cirrostratus, altostratus, and nimbostratus, are formed while the pressure is decreasing.

Thick rain clouds

Rain below the front

A barely noticeable imbalance of a warm front

As the clouds extend over a region, they produce light rain or snow.

The mass of cold air takes the form of a retreating wedge, which has the effect of lifting the warm air as it moves over the mass of cold air.

If the warm front moves faster than the retreating wedge of cold air, the height of the advancing warm front continues to increase.

Colors in the Sky

A natural spectacle of incomparable beauty, the auroras are produced around the magnetic poles of the Earth by the activity of the Sun. Solar wind acts on the magnetosphere, which is a part of the exosphere. In general, the greater the solar wind, the more prominent the aurora. Auroras consist of luminous patches and columns of various colors. Depending on whether they appear in the north or south, they are called aurora borealis or aurora australis. The aurora borealis can be seen in Alaska, Canada, and the Scandinavian countries.

NORTH POLE

A satellite image of the aurora borealis

Solar Winds

The Sun emits radiation, continuously and in all directions. This radiation occurs as a flow of charged particles or plasma, which consists mainly of electrons and protons. The plasma particles are guided by the magnetic field of the Sun and form the solar wind, which travels through space at some 275 miles per second (450 km/s). Particles from the solar wind arrive at the Earth within four or five days

BOW SHOCK WAVE

SOLAR WIND

THE SUN emits solar winds, which cause serious damage and an increase in temperature.

MAGNETOTAIL

How They Are Produced

➡️ The auroras are the result of the shock produced as ions coming from the Sun make contact with the magnetic field of the Earth. They appear in different colors depending on the altitude at which they are produced. Moreover, they demonstrate the function of the magnetosphere, which protects the planet against solar winds.

620 miles
(1,000 km)

is how long an aurora can be. From space it will look like a circle around one of the magnetic poles of the Earth.

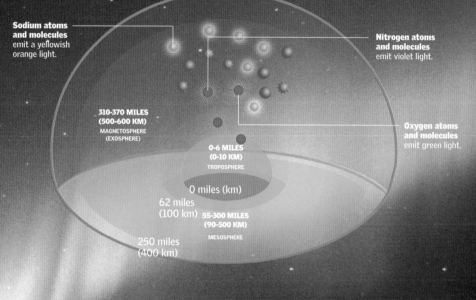

Sodium atoms and molecules emit a yellowish orange light.

Nitrogen atoms and molecules emit violet light.

310-370 MILES (500-600 KM) MAGNETOSPHERE (EXOSPHERE)

Oxygen atoms and molecules emit green light.

0-6 MILES (0-10 KM) TROPOSPHERE

0 miles (km)

62 miles (100 km)

55-300 MILES (90-500 KM) MESOSPHERE

250 miles (400 km)

1 ELECTRONS COLLIDE WITH MOLECULES
The oxygen and nitrogen molecules receive the impact of the particles from the Sun. This occurs in the magnetosphere (exosphere).

2 THEY BECOME EXCITED
After the shock, the atoms receive a significant additional energetic charge that will be released in the form of photons (light).

3 THEY GENERATE LIGHT
Depending on the altitude and the velocity where the shock is produced, the aurora displays different colors. Among the possibilities are violet, green, orange, and yellow.

10-20 minutes
duration of the phenomenon

The amount of light emitted oscillates between 1 and 10 million megawatts, equivalent to the energy produced by 1,000 to 10,000 large electric power plants.

THE EARTH
The Earth's magnetosphere is responsible for protecting the planet from the deadly and harmful solar winds.

THE POLES
The auroras are more noticeable near the poles; they are called aurora borealis in the Northern Hemisphere and aurora australis in the Southern Hemisphere.

OVAL AURORA

Surface Factors

A mong meteorological phenomena, rain plays a very important role in the life of humans. Its scarcity causes serious problems, such as droughts, lack of food, and an increase in infant mortality. It is clear that an excess of water, caused by overabundant rain or the effects of gigantic waves, is also cause for alarm and concern. In

VIETNAM, DECEMBER 1991
The intense monsoon rains
caused severe flooding in vast
regions of Cambodia, Vietnam,
Laos, and Thailand.

LIVING WATER 20-21

OCEAN CURRENTS 22-23

AN OBSTACLE COURSE 24-25

THE LAND AND THE OCEAN 26-27

MONSOONS 28-29

GOOD FORTUNE AND CATASTROPHE 30-31

THE ARRIVAL OF EL NIÑO 32-33

THE EFFECTS OF EL NIÑO 34-35

Southwest Asia, there are frequent typhoons and torrential rains during which millions of people lose their houses and must be relocated to more secure areas; however, they still run the risk of catching contagious diseases such as malaria. The warm current of El Niño also affects the lives and the economy of millions of people. ●

Living Water

The water in the oceans, rivers, clouds, and rain is in constant motion. Surface water evaporates, water in the clouds precipitates, and this precipitation runs along and seeps into the Earth. Nonetheless, the total amount of water on the planet does not change. The circulation and conservation of water is driven by the hydrologic, or water, cycle. This cycle begins with evaporation of water from the Earth's surface. The water vapor humidifies as the air rises. The water vapor in the air cools and condenses onto solid particles as microdroplets. The microdroplets combine to form clouds. When the droplets become large enough, they begin to fall back to Earth, and, depending on the temperature of the atmosphere, they return to the ground as rain, snow, or hail. ●

1. EVAPORATION
Thanks to the effects of the Sun, ocean water is warmed and fills the air with water vapor. Evaporation from humid soil and vegetation increases humidity. The result is the formation of clouds.

TRANSPIRATION
Perspiration is a natural process that regulates body temperature. When the body temperature rises, the sweat glands are stimulated, causing perspiration.

CONTRIBUTION OF LIVING BEINGS, ESPECIALLY PLANTS, TO

10%
THE WATER IN THE ATMOSPHERE

THE HUMAN BODY IS **65% WATER.**

2. CONDENSATION
In order for water vapor to condense and form clouds, the air must contain condensation nuclei, which allow the molecules of water to form microdroplets. For condensation to occur, the water must be cooled.

FORMATION OF DROPLETS
The molecules of water vapor decrease their mobility and begin to collect on solid particles suspended in the air.

Nucleus

GASEOUS STATE
The rays of the Sun increase the motion of atmospheric gases. The combination of heat and wind transforms liquid water into water vapor.

3 The water vapor escapes via micropores in the leaves' surface.

2 The water ascends via the stem.

1 The root absorbs water.

Root cells

CLOUDS

All the molecules of water are freed.

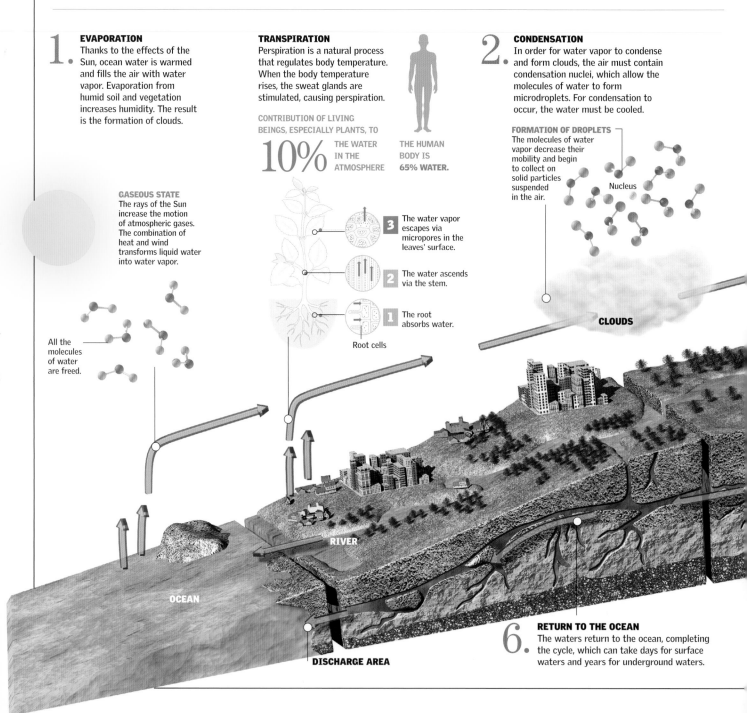

OCEAN

RIVER

6. RETURN TO THE OCEAN
The waters return to the ocean, completing the cycle, which can take days for surface waters and years for underground waters.

DISCHARGE AREA

WATER AVAILABILITY

(cubic feet [cu m]
per capita/year)

- ■ Less than 60,000 cu ft
  (1,700 cu m)
- ▨ 60,000-175,000 cu ft
  (1,700-5,000 cu m)
- ■ More than 175,000 cu ft
  (5,000 cu m)

Access to potable water

- ▨ Less than 50% of the
  population

Arctic Ocean
North America
Europe
Asia
Atlantic Ocean
Pacific Ocean
Pacific Ocean
Africa
Indian Ocean
South America
Oceania

WHERE IT IS FOUND

FRESHWATER   SALT WATER

A small percentage is
freshwater; most of it
is salt water.

3% 97%

FRESHWATER

Underground water **1%**

Ice **2%**

0.03%
water on
the surface
and in the
atmosphere

Lakes **0.029%**

Atmosphere **0.001%**

Rivers **0.00015%**

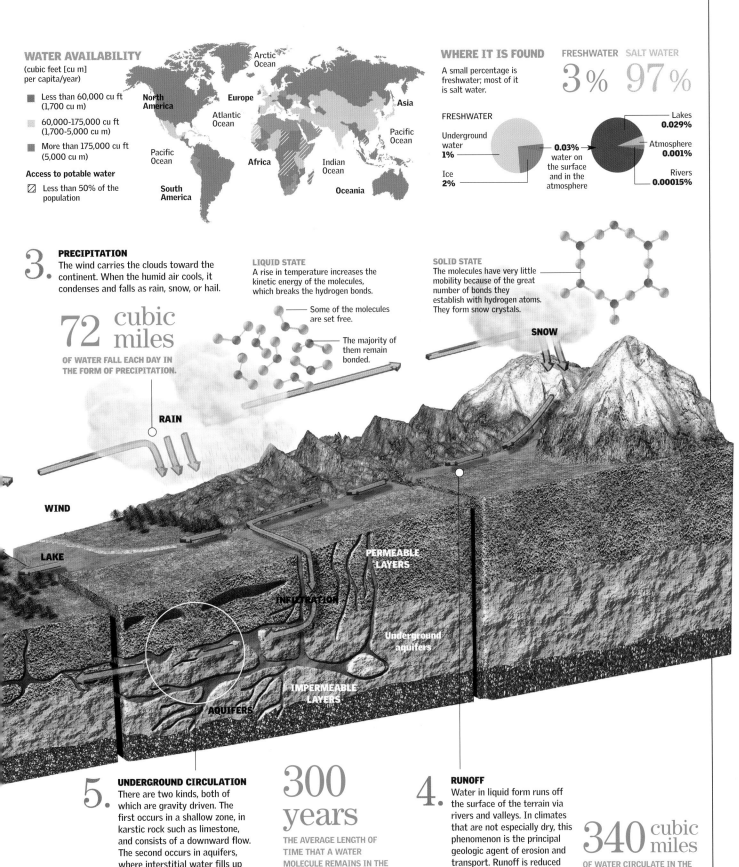

3. PRECIPITATION

The wind carries the clouds toward the
continent. When the humid air cools, it
condenses and falls as rain, snow, or hail.

LIQUID STATE
A rise in temperature increases the
kinetic energy of the molecules,
which breaks the hydrogen bonds.

Some of the molecules
are set free.

The majority of
them remain
bonded.

SOLID STATE
The molecules have very little
mobility because of the great
number of bonds they
establish with hydrogen atoms.
They form snow crystals.

SNOW

72 cubic miles

**OF WATER FALL EACH DAY IN
THE FORM OF PRECIPITATION.**

RAIN

WIND

LAKE

PERMEABLE LAYERS

INFILTRATION

Underground aquifers

AQUIFERS

IMPERMEABLE LAYERS

5. UNDERGROUND CIRCULATION

There are two kinds, both of
which are gravity driven. The
first occurs in a shallow zone, in
karstic rock such as limestone,
and consists of a downward flow.
The second occurs in aquifers,
where interstitial water fills up
the pores of a rock.

300 years

**THE AVERAGE LENGTH OF
TIME THAT A WATER
MOLECULE REMAINS IN THE
UNDERGROUND AQUIFERS**

4. RUNOFF

Water in liquid form runs off
the surface of the terrain via
rivers and valleys. In climates
that are not especially dry, this
phenomenon is the principal
geologic agent of erosion and
transport. Runoff is reduced
during times of drought.

340 cubic miles

**OF WATER CIRCULATE IN THE
TERRESTRIAL HYDROSPHERE.**

Ocean Currents

Ocean water moves as waves, tides, and currents. There are two types of currents: surface and deep. The surface currents, caused by the wind, are great rivers in the ocean. They can be some 50 miles (80 km) wide. They have a profound effect on the world climate because the water warms up near the Equator, and currents transfer this heat to higher latitudes. Deep currents are caused by differences in water density.●

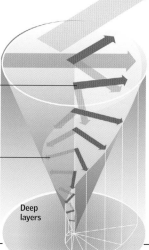

Alaska

North Pacific Current

Pacific Ocean

California Current

Labra...

Gulf Stream

Atlantic Ocean

North Equatorial Countercurrent

Canary Current

Equatorial Countercurrent

North Equatorial Countercurrent

South Equatorial Current

Equatorial Counterc...

South Equa...

Peruvian Current

Brazil Current

Atla Ocea

Pacific Ocean

Falkland Current

Antarctic Circumpolar Current

THE INFLUENCE OF THE WINDS

TIDES AND THE CORIOLIS EFFECT

The Coriolis effect, which influences the direction of the winds, drives the displacement of marine currents.

Currents in the Northern Hemisphere travel in a clockwise direction.

In the Southern Hemisphere, the currents travel in a counterclockwise direction.

GEOSTROPHIC BALANCE

The deflection caused by the Coriolis effect on the currents is compensated for by pressure gradients between cyclonic and anticyclonic systems. This effect is called geostrophic balance.

Coriolis force

Pressure gradient

Winds

High pressure
Subtropical high-pressure center

Low pressure
Subpolar low pressure

HOW CURRENTS ARE FORMED

Wind and solar energy produce surface currents in the water.

1. In the Southern Hemisphere, coastal winds push away the surface water so that cold water can ascend.

2. This slow ascent of deep water is called a surge. This motion is modified by the Ekman spiral effect.

COAST

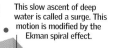

Warm surface waters

Subsurface waters occupy the space left by the motion of the surface waters.

64° F (18 °C)

61° F (16 °C)

57° F (14 °C)

54° F (12 °C)

Deep cold water

EKMAN SPIRAL

explains why the surface currents and deep currents are opposite in direction.

Wind energy is transferred to the water in **friction layers**. Thus, the velocity of the surface water increases more than that of the deep water.

The Coriolis effect causes the **direction of the currents** to deviate. The surface currents travel in the opposite direction of the deep currents.

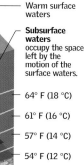

Deep layers

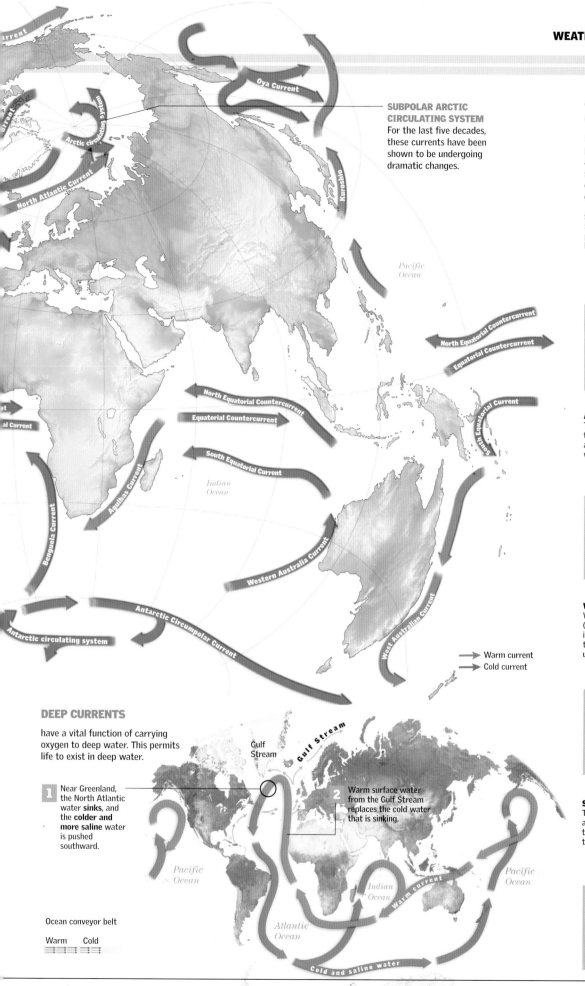

Oya Current

Arctic circulating system

North Atlantic Current

Kuroshio

Pacific Ocean

North Equatorial Countercurrent

Equatorial Countercurrent

North Equatorial Countercurrent

Equatorial Countercurrent

South Equatorial Current

South Equatorial Current

Aguihas Current

Benguela Current

Indian Ocean

Western Australia Current

West Australian Current

Antarctic Circumpolar Current

Antarctic circulating system

→ Warm current
→ Cold current

SUBPOLAR ARCTIC CIRCULATING SYSTEM
For the last five decades, these currents have been shown to be undergoing dramatic changes.

THE FOUR SEASONS OF A LAKE

Because of the physical properties of water, lakes and lagoons have a special seasonal circulation that ensures the survival of living creatures.

SUMMER
Stable summer temperatures prevent vertical circulation in the body of water of the lagoon.

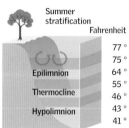

Summer stratification

Fahrenheit

	77°
	75°
Epilimnion	64°
	55°
Thermocline	46°
Hypolimnion	43°
	41°

AUTUMN
Temperature decrease and temperature variations generate a mixing of the surface and deep waters.

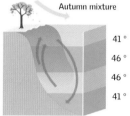

Autumn mixture

41°
46°
46°
41°

WINTER
When the water reaches 39° F (4° C), its density increases. That is how strata of solid water on the surface and liquid water underneath are created.

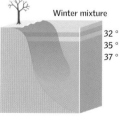

Winter mixture

32°
35°
37°

SPRING
The characteristics of water once again initiate vertical circulation in the lake. Spring temperatures lead to this circulation.

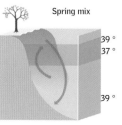

Spring mix

39°
37°
39°

DEEP CURRENTS

have a vital function of carrying oxygen to deep water. This permits life to exist in deep water.

1 Near Greenland, the North Atlantic water **sinks**, and the **colder and more saline** water is pushed southward.

Gulf Stream

Gulf Stream

2 Warm surface water from the Gulf Stream replaces the cold water that is sinking.

Pacific Ocean

Indian Ocean

Warm current

Pacific Ocean

Atlantic Ocean

Cold and saline water

Ocean conveyor belt

Warm   Cold

An Obstacle Course

The mountains are geographical features with a great influence on climate. Winds laden with moisture collide with these vertical obstacles and have to rise up their slopes to pass over them. During the ascent, the air discharges water in the form of precipitation on the windward sides, which are humid and have dense vegetation. The air that reaches the leeward slopes is dry, and the vegetation usually consists of sparse grazing land. ●

The Effect of the Andes Mountains

1. HUMID WINDS
In the mountains, the predominant winds are moisture-laden and blow in the direction of the coastal mountains.

2. ASCENT AND CONDENSATION
Condensation occurs when a mass of air cools until it reaches the saturation point (relative humidity 100 percent). The dew point rises when the air becomes saturated as it cools and the pressure is held constant.

3. PRECIPITATION
A natural barrier forces the air to ascend and cool. The result is cloud formation and precipitation.

IN THE CLOUD

Temperature (in °F [°C])	Composition
-40 to -4 (-40 to -20)	Ice crystals
-4 to 14 (-20 to -10)	Supercooled water
14 to 32 (-10 to 0)	Microdroplets of water
Greater than 32 (0)	Drops of water

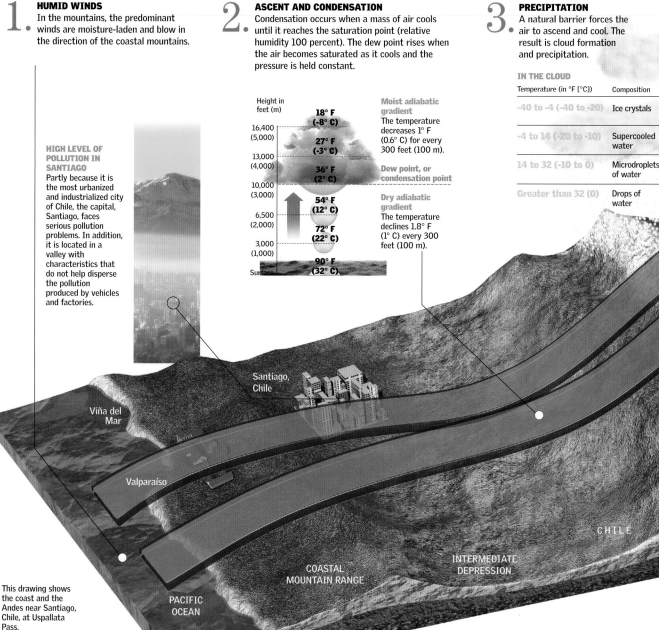

HIGH LEVEL OF POLLUTION IN SANTIAGO
Partly because it is the most urbanized and industrialized city of Chile, the capital, Santiago, faces serious pollution problems. In addition, it is located in a valley with characteristics that do not help disperse the pollution produced by vehicles and factories.

Height in feet (m)

16,400 (5,000) — 18° F (-8° C)

13,000 (4,000) — 27° F (-3° C)

10,000 (3,000) — 36° F (2° C)

6,500 (2,000) — 54° F (12° C)

3,000 (1,000) — 72° F (22° C)

Surface — 90° F (32° C)

Moist adiabatic gradient
The temperature decreases 1° F (0.6° C) for every 300 feet (100 m).

Dew point, or condensation point

Dry adiabatic gradient
The temperature declines 1.8° F (1° C) every 300 feet (100 m).

Viña del Mar

Santiago, Chile

Valparaíso

PACIFIC OCEAN

COASTAL MOUNTAIN RANGE

INTERMEDIATE DEPRESSION

CHILE

This drawing shows the coast and the Andes near Santiago, Chile, at Uspallata Pass.

MAJOR MOUNTAIN RANGES

Rocky Mountains
Urals
Alps
Himalayas
Appalachians
Andes

Mountain	Elevation
Everest	29,035 feet (8,850 m)
Aconcagua	22,834 feet (6,960 m)
Dhaulagiri	26,795 feet (8,167 m)
Makalu	27,766 feet (8,463 m)
Nanga Parbat	26,660 feet (8,126 m)
Kanchenjunga	28,169 feet (8,586 m)
Ojos del Salado	22,614 feet (6,893 m)
Kilimanjaro	19,340 feet (5,895 m)

VEGETATION

13,000 (4,000)
10,000 (3,000)
6,500 (2,000)
3,000 (1,000)
0 feet (0 m)

Tundra. Its rate of growth is slow and only during the summer.

Taiga. The vegetation is conifer forest.

Mixed forest. Made up of deciduous trees and conifers.

Chaparral. Brush with thick and dry leaves.

Grazing. Thickets predominate: low, perennial grazing plants with an herbaceous appearance.

SNOW
Drops of super-cooled water combine to form ice crystals.

The crystals grow in size.

While they are falling, they combine with other crystals.

RAIN
The microdroplets increase in size and fall because of gravity.

When they fall, these drops collide with smaller ones.

Successive collisions increase the size of the drops.

4. DESCENDING WIND
A natural barrier forces the air to descend and warm up.

Western slopes receive most of the moisture, which leads to the growth of pine and other trees of coastal mountain ranges.

Eastern slopes The rays of the Sun fall directly upon these areas, making them more arid. There is little or no vegetation.

HOW OBSTACLES WORK

Obstacles, such as buildings, trees, and rock formations, decrease the velocity of the wind significantly and often create turbulence around them.

FRONT VIEW — Rotational flow

PLAN VIEW — Flow and counterflow

ANDES MOUNTAIN RANGE has altitudes greater than

19,700 feet (6,000 m).

It runs parallel to the Pacific Ocean, from Panama to southern Argentina. It is 4,500 miles (7,240 km) long and 150 miles (241 km) wide.

ARGENTINA

TYPES OF OROGRAPHICAL EFFECTS

DRY Winds
HUMIDS Winds
Area affected by precipitation

CLASSIC SCHEME
The more humid zone is at the top.

VERY HIGH
This is produced on mountains above 16,400 feet (5,000 m) in height.

The most humid area is halfway up the slope, on the windward side.

UNEVEN MOUNTAINSIDE
The most humid area is at the top of the leeward slope.

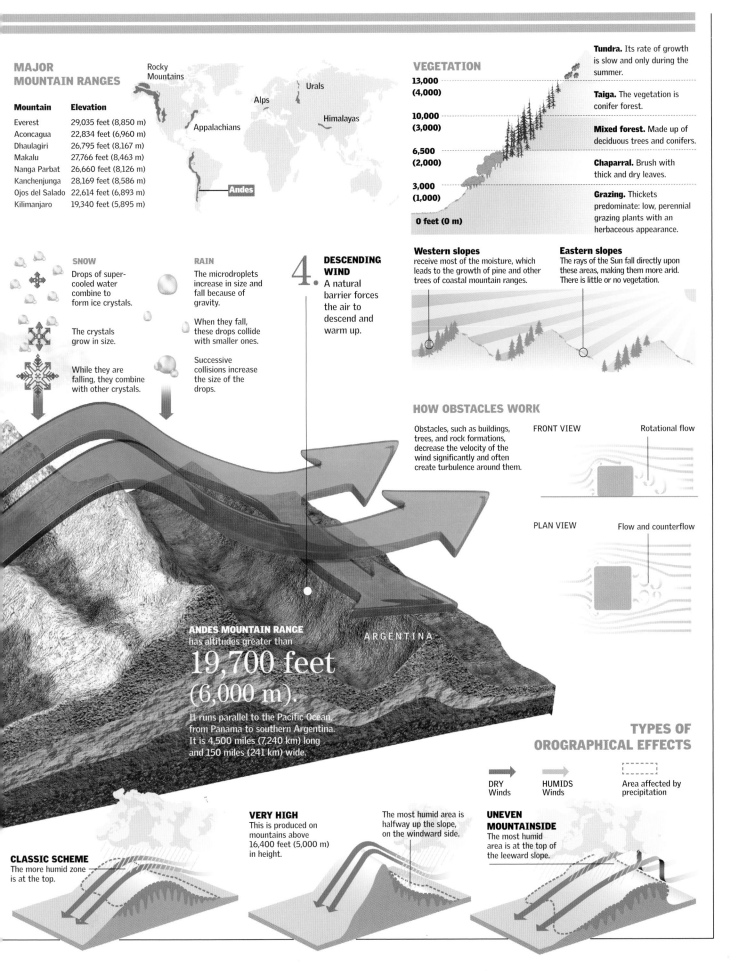

The Land and the Ocean

Temperature distribution and, above all, temperature differences very much depend on the distribution of land and water surface. Differences in specific heat moderate the temperatures of regions close to great masses of water. Water absorbs heat and releases it more slowly than the land does, which is why a body of water can heat or cool the environment. Its influence is unmistakable. Moreover, these differences between the land and the sea are the cause of the coastal winds. In clear weather, the land heats up during the day, which causes the air to rise rapidly and form a low-pressure zone. This zone draws marine breezes. ●

WINDS OF THE MOUNTAINS AND VALLEYS

1 The Sun heats the soil of the valley and the surrounding air, which ascends by convection.

2 The air is cooled as it ascends, becomes more dense, and descends. Then it heats up again and repeats the cycle.

VALLEY

80%
RECENT SNOW

SLOPE

75%
THICK CLOUDS

DAY

15%
ALBEDO OF MEADOWS

ABSORPTION OF HEAT

1 Cold air currents descend from the mountainside toward the floor of the valley, which is still hot.

2 The air currents are heated and ascend by convection. When they rise, they cool and once again descend along the mountainside.

MOUNTAINSIDE

VALLEY

NIGHT

RELEASE OF HEAT

MOUNTAIN WINDS

Chinook WINDS

These winds are dry and warm, sometimes quite hot, occurring in various places of the world. In the western United States, they are called chinooks and are capable of making snow disappear within minutes.

Humid winds are lifted over the slopes, creating clouds and precipitation on the windward side. These are called anabatic winds.

The dry and cool wind descends down the mountain slope on the leeward side. It is called katabatic.

LEEWARD

WINDWARD

WARM AIR WHIRLWINDS

Intense heat on the plains can generate a hot, spiral-formed column of air sometimes more than 300 feet (100 m) high.

1 1 Strong, high-speed winds move on top of weaker winds and cause the **intermediate air to be displaced like a pencil on a table.**

2 A powerful air current lifts the spiral.

STRONG WIND

MILD WIND

Winds	Characteristics	Location
Autan wind	Dry and mild	Southwestern France
Berg	Dry and warm	South Africa
Bora	Dry and cold	Northeastern Italy
Brickfielder	Dry and hot	Australia
Buran	Dry and cold	Mongolia
Harmattan	Dry and cool	North Africa
Levant	Humid and mild	Mediterranean region
Mistral	Dry and cold	Rhône valley
Santa Ana	Dry and hot	Southern California
Sirocco	Dry and hot	Southern Europe and North Africa
Tramontana	Dry and cold	Northeast Spain
Zonda	Dry and mild	Western Argentina

HEAT ISLANDS

Cities are complex surfaces. Concrete and asphalt absorb a large quantity of heat during sunny days and release it during the night.

Isotherms in a typical city

81°F — 81°F
82°F — 82°F
84°F — 84°F
84°F — 84°F
82°F — 82°F

84°F 86°F 88°F   90°F 86°F 82°F
82°F 90°F   88°F 84°F

CONTINENTALITY

In the interior of a landmass, there is a wide variation of daily temperatures, while on the coasts, the influence of the ocean reduces this variation. This continentality effect is quite noticeable in the United States, Russia, India, and Australia.

Daily variation of temperatures in the United States

Continentality index

Less   More

+ ALBEDO → – ENERGY ABSORBED

25% WET SAND

3-5% WATER (WHEN THE SUN IS HIGH)

50% LIGHT CLOUDS

7-14% FORESTS

They absorb a significant amount of heat but remain cool because much energy is used to evaporate the moisture.

COASTAL BREEZES

1.

ON THE LAND
During the day, the land heats up more rapidly than the ocean. The warm air rises and is replaced by cooler air coming from the sea.

LAND

WARM AIR

Because it is opaque, the heat stays in the **surface layers**, which are heated and cooled rapidly.

IN THE OCEAN
From the coast, the ocean receives air that loses its heat near the water. As a result, the colder air descends toward the sea.

COLD AIR

WATER

The heat penetrates into **deeper layers** thanks to the transparency of the water. A part of the heat is lost in evaporation of the water.

Factories and vehicles emit large amounts of heat into the atmosphere.

SEA BREEZE

The air tends to descend in forested and rural areas.

During the night, the city slowly releases heat that was absorbed during the day.

The flows tend toward equilibrium.

2.

ON THE LAND
During the evening, the land radiates away its heat more rapidly than the water. The difference in pressure generated replaces the cold air of the coast with warm air.

COLD AIR

LAND

When night falls, the land, which was hot, **cools rapidly.**

IN THE OCEAN
The loss of heat from the water is slower.

WARM AIR

WATER

When night falls, the water is **lukewarm** (barely a degree more than the land).

LAND BREEZE

KEY

WARM-AIR FLOW

COLD-AIR FLOW

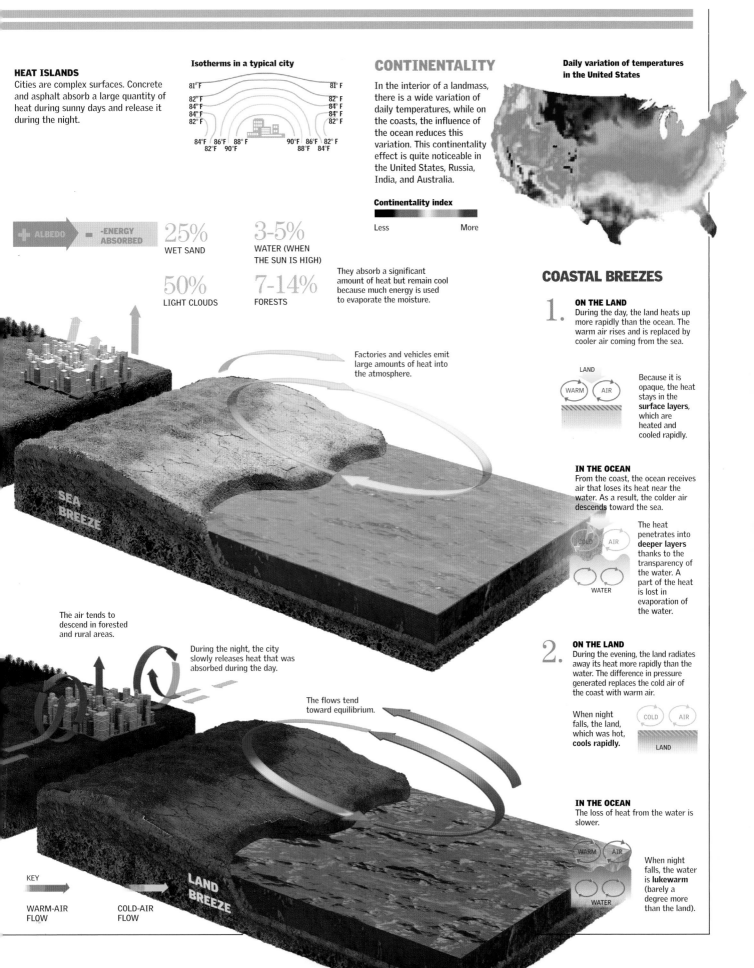

Monsoons

The strong humid winds that usually affect the tropical zone are called monsoons, an Arabic word meaning "seasonal winds." During summer in the Northern Hemisphere, they blow across Southeast Asia, especially the Indian peninsula. Conditions change in the winter, and the winds reverse and shift toward the northern regions of Australia. This phenomenon, which is also frequent in continental areas of the United States, is part of an annual cycle that, as a result of its intensity and its consequences, affects the lives of many people. ●

AREAS AFFECTED BY MONSOONS

This phenomenon affects the climates in low latitudes, from West Africa to the western Pacific. In the summer, the monsoon causes the rains in the Amazon region and in northern Argentina. There in the winter rain is usually scarce.

Predominant direction of the winds during the month of July

THE MONSOON OF NORTH AMERICA

Pre-monsoon. Month of May.

Monsoon. Month of July.

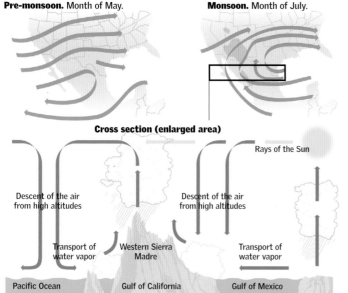

Cross section (enlarged area)

Rays of the Sun

Descent of the air from high altitudes

Descent of the air from high altitudes

Transport of water vapor

Western Sierra Madre

Transport of water vapor

Pacific Ocean

Gulf of California

Gulf of Mexico

How monsoons are created in India

End of the monsoon	Beginning of the monsoon	Cold and dry winds	Cold and humid winds	Cyclone (low pressure)	Anticyclone (high pressure)

1 THE CONTINENT COOLS

After the summer monsoon, the rains stop and temperatures in Central and South Asia begin to drop. Winter begins in the Northern Hemisphere.

Northern Hemisphere
It is winter. The rays of the Sun are oblique, traveling a longer distance through the atmosphere to reach the Earth's surface. Thus they are spread over a larger surface, so the average temperature is lower than in the Southern Hemisphere.

Rays of the Sun

Southern Hemisphere
It is summer. The rays of the Sun strike the surface at a right angle; they are concentrated in a smaller area, so the temperature on average is higher than in the Northern Hemisphere.

2 FROM THE CONTINENT TO THE OCEAN

The masses of cold and dry air that predominate on the continent are displaced toward the ocean, whose waters are relatively warmer.

Arabian Sea

3 OCEAN STORMS

A cyclone located in the ocean draws the cold winds from the continent and lifts the somewhat warmer and more humid air, which returns toward the continent via the upper layers of the atmosphere.

INTERTROPICAL INFLUENCE

The circulation of the atmosphere between the tropics influences the formation of monsoon winds. The trade winds that blow toward the Equator from the subtropical zones are pushed by the Hadley cells and deflected in their course by the Coriolis effect. Winds in the tropics occur within a band of low pressure around the Earth called the Intertropical Convergence Zone (ITCZ). When this zone is seasonally displaced in the warm months of the Northern Hemisphere toward the north, a summer monsoon occurs.

Limit of the Intertropical Convergence Zone (ITCZ)

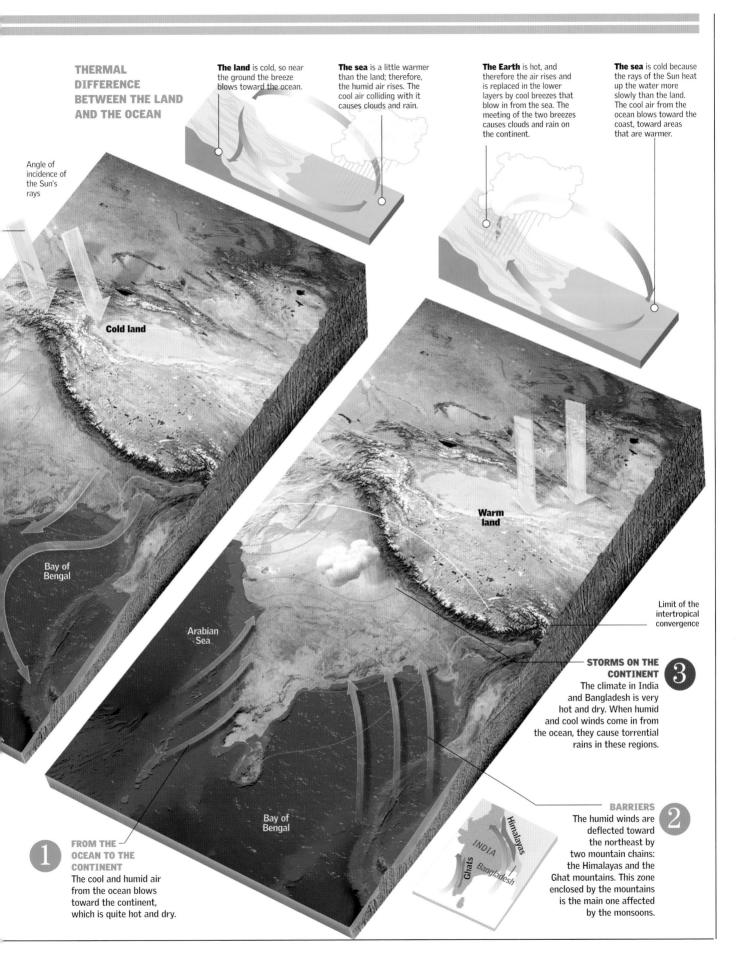

THERMAL
DIFFERENCE
BETWEEN THE LAND
AND THE OCEAN

The land is cold, so near the ground the breeze blows toward the ocean.

The sea is a little warmer than the land; therefore, the humid air rises. The cool air colliding with it causes clouds and rain.

The Earth is hot, and therefore the air rises and is replaced in the lower layers by cool breezes that blow in from the sea. The meeting of the two breezes causes clouds and rain on the continent.

The sea is cold because the rays of the Sun heat up the water more slowly than the land. The cool air from the ocean blows toward the coast, toward areas that are warmer.

Angle of incidence of the Sun's rays

Cold land

Bay of Bengal

Arabian Sea

Warm land

Limit of the intertropical convergence

Bay of Bengal

STORMS ON THE CONTINENT ③
The climate in India and Bangladesh is very hot and dry. When humid and cool winds come in from the ocean, they cause torrential rains in these regions.

Himalayas

INDIA

Ghats Bangladesh

FROM THE OCEAN TO THE CONTINENT ①
The cool and humid air from the ocean blows toward the continent, which is quite hot and dry.

BARRIERS ②
The humid winds are deflected toward the northeast by two mountain chains: the Himalayas and the Ghat mountains. This zone enclosed by the mountains is the main one affected by the monsoons.

Good Fortune and Catastrophe

The monsoons are a climatic phenomenon governing the life and the economy of one of the most densely populated regions of the planet, especially India. The arrival of the intense rains is celebrated as the end of a season that might have been extremely dry, but it is also feared. The flooding at times devastates agriculture and housing. The damage is even greater because of the large population of the region. Therefore, anticipating disaster and taking precautions, such as evacuating areas prone to flooding, are part of the organization of agricultural activity, which thrives in periods of heavy rains, even in fields that are flooded.

UNDERWATER HARVEST
The mud increases the fertility of the soil, which compensates for the losses. The accumulation of humid sand is later used in the dry season. Rice is a grain that grows in fields that are underwater.

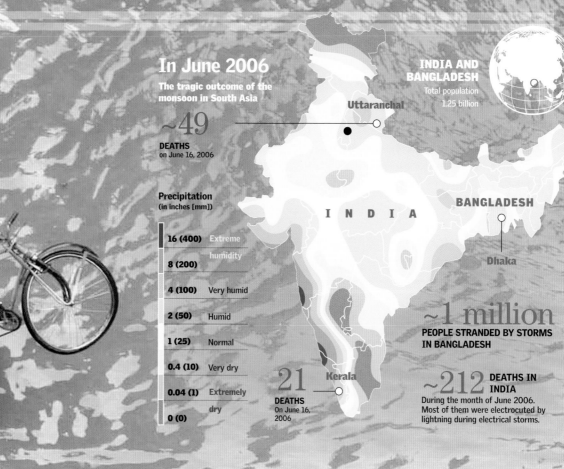

In June 2006

The tragic outcome of the monsoon in South Asia

~49

DEATHS
on June 16, 2006

INDIA AND BANGLADESH
Total population
1.25 billion

Precipitation
(in inches [mm])

16 (400)	Extreme
8 (200)	humidity
4 (100)	Very humid
2 (50)	Humid
1 (25)	Normal
0.4 (10)	Very dry
0.04 (1)	Extremely
0 (0)	dry

~1 million
PEOPLE STRANDED BY STORMS IN BANGLADESH

21
DEATHS
On June 16, 2006

~212 **DEATHS IN INDIA**
During the month of June 2006. Most of them were electrocuted by lightning during electrical storms.

Uttaranchal

INDIA

BANGLADESH

Dhaka

Kerala

OVERFLOWING RIVERS
The valley that connects the Ganges with the Brahmaputra in Bangladesh is the most afflicted by floods caused by these rains. The rains destroy harvests and property.

The Arrival of El Niño

The hydrosphere and the atmosphere interact and establish a dynamic thermal equilibrium between the water and the air. If this balance is altered, unusual climatic phenomena occur between the coasts of Peru and Southeast Asia. For example, the phenomenon El Niño or, less frequently, another phenomenon called La Niña are responsible for atypical droughts and floods that every two to seven years affect the routine life of people living on these Pacific Ocean coasts. ●

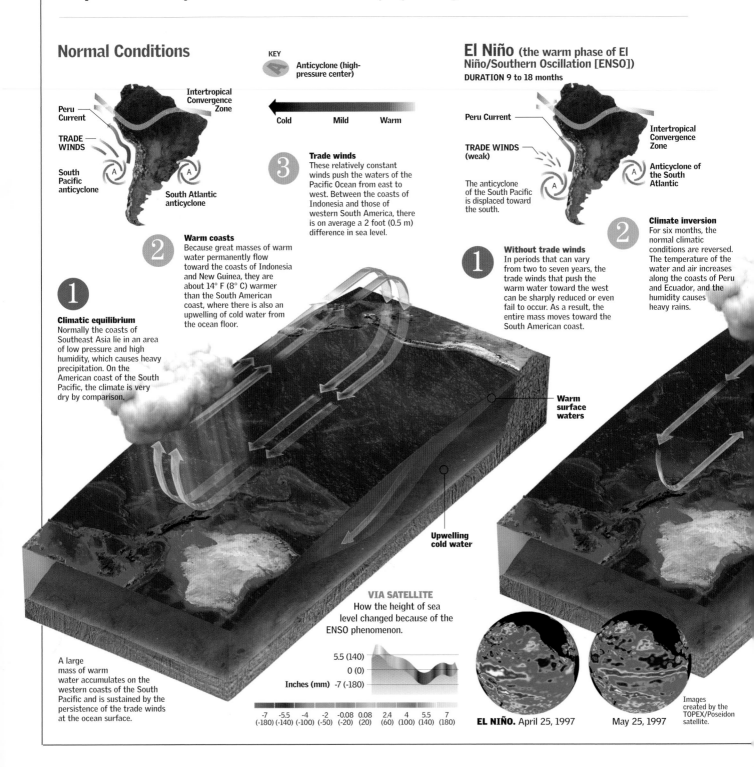

Normal Conditions

KEY

Anticyclone (high-pressure center)

Cold — Mild — Warm

Intertropical Convergence Zone

Peru Current

TRADE WINDS

South Pacific anticyclone

South Atlantic anticyclone

3 Trade winds
These relatively constant winds push the waters of the Pacific Ocean from east to west. Between the coasts of Indonesia and those of western South America, there is on average a 2 foot (0.5 m) difference in sea level.

2 Warm coasts
Because great masses of warm water permanently flow toward the coasts of Indonesia and New Guinea, they are about 14° F (8° C) warmer than the South American coast, where there is also an upwelling of cold water from the ocean floor.

1 Climatic equilibrium
Normally the coasts of Southeast Asia lie in an area of low pressure and high humidity, which causes heavy precipitation. On the American coast of the South Pacific, the climate is very dry by comparison.

A large mass of warm water accumulates on the western coasts of the South Pacific and is sustained by the persistence of the trade winds at the ocean surface.

El Niño (the warm phase of El Niño/Southern Oscillation [ENSO])
DURATION 9 to 18 months

Peru Current

TRADE WINDS (weak)

The anticyclone of the South Pacific is displaced toward the south.

Intertropical Convergence Zone

Anticyclone of the South Atlantic

2 Climate inversion
For six months, the normal climatic conditions are reversed. The temperature of the water and air increases along the coasts of Peru and Ecuador, and the humidity causes heavy rains.

1 Without trade winds
In periods that can vary from two to seven years, the trade winds that push the warm water toward the west can be sharply reduced or even fail to occur. As a result, the entire mass moves toward the South American coast.

Warm surface waters

Upwelling cold water

VIA SATELLITE
How the height of sea level changed because of the ENSO phenomenon.

5.5 (140)
0 (0)
Inches (mm) -7 (-180)

-7 (-180) | -5.5 (-140) | -4 (-100) | -2 (-50) | -0.08 (-20) | 0.08 (20) | 2.4 (60) | 4 (100) | 5.5 (140) | 7 (180)

EL NIÑO. April 25, 1997   May 25, 1997

Images created by the TOPEX/Poseidon satellite.

SURFACE TEMPERATURE OF THE OCEAN

The graphic shows the temperature variations caused by the Southern Oscillation in the water along the coast of Peru. This graphic illustrates the alternation of the El Niño and La Niña phenomena over the last 50 years.

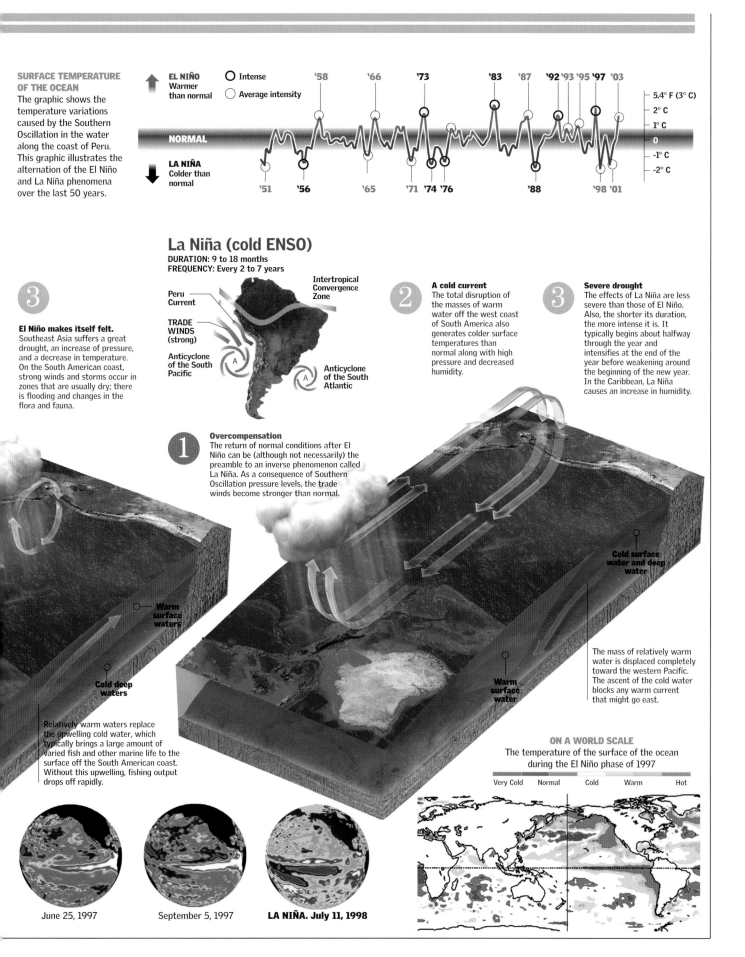

EL NIÑO Warmer than normal

○ Intense
○ Average intensity

'58 '66 **'73** '83 '87 **'92** '93 '95 **'97** '03

NORMAL

5.4° F (3° C)
2° C
1° C
0
-1° C
-2° C

LA NIÑA Colder than normal

'51 **'56** '65 '71 **'74 '76** '88 '98 '01

La Niña (cold ENSO)
DURATION: 9 to 18 months
FREQUENCY: Every 2 to 7 years

Intertropical Convergence Zone

Peru Current

TRADE WINDS (strong)

Anticyclone of the South Pacific

A

Anticyclone of the South Atlantic

A

3

El Niño makes itself felt.
Southeast Asia suffers a great drought, an increase of pressure, and a decrease in temperature. On the South American coast, strong winds and storms occur in zones that are usually dry; there is flooding and changes in the flora and fauna.

2

A cold current
The total disruption of the masses of warm water off the west coast of South America also generates colder surface temperatures than normal along with high pressure and decreased humidity.

3

Severe drought
The effects of La Niña are less severe than those of El Niño. Also, the shorter its duration, the more intense it is. It typically begins about halfway through the year and intensifies at the end of the year before weakening around the beginning of the new year. In the Caribbean, La Niña causes an increase in humidity.

1

Overcompensation
The return of normal conditions after El Niño can be (although not necessarily) the preamble to an inverse phenomenon called La Niña. As a consequence of Southern Oscillation pressure levels, the trade winds become stronger than normal.

Cold surface water and deep water

Warm surface waters

Cold deep waters

Warm surface water

The mass of relatively warm water is displaced completely toward the western Pacific. The ascent of the cold water blocks any warm current that might go east.

Relatively warm waters replace the upwelling cold water, which typically brings a large amount of varied fish and other marine life to the surface off the South American coast. Without this upwelling, fishing output drops off rapidly.

ON A WORLD SCALE
The temperature of the surface of the ocean during the El Niño phase of 1997

Very Cold | Normal | Cold | Warm | Hot

June 25, 1997

September 5, 1997

LA NIÑA. July 11, 1998

The Effects of El Niño

The natural warm phenomenon known as El Niño alters the temperature of the water within the east central zone of the Pacific Ocean along the coasts of Ecuador and Peru. Farmers and fishermen are negatively affected by these changes in temperature and the modification of marine currents. The nutrients normally present in the ocean decrease or disappear from along the coast because of the increase in temperature. As the entire food chain deteriorates, other species also suffer the effects and disappear from the ocean. In contrast, tropical marine species that live in warmer waters can flourish. The phenomenon affects the weather and climate of the entire world. It tends to cause flooding, food shortages, droughts, and fires in various locations. ●

FLOODING
Abnormal flooding caused by El Niño in the desert regions of Chile and the later evaporation of water leave behind hexagonal deposits of potassium nitrate.

ATACAMA, CHILE
Laguna Blanca
Salt Marsh
Latitude 22° 54´ S
Longitude 68° 12´ W

Surface area	**1,200 square miles (3,000 sq km)**
Cause	**Floods caused by El Niño anomalies**
Year	**1999**

Areas Affected

EL NIÑO from December to February

LA NIÑA from June to August

ASIA

AMERICA

AFRICA

OCEANIA

ASIA

AMERICA

AFRICA

OCEANIA

Normal conditions
Cold waters, rich in nutrients, ascend from the bottom of the sea and provide favorable conditions for the growth of phytoplankton, the basis of the marine food chain.

The phytoplankton promote the normal development of microorganisms, fish, and other creatures.

During El Niño,
the scarcity of cold water debilitates the phytoplankton population and alters the marine food chain.

Various marine species die off for lack of food or must migrate to other zones.

Meteorological Phenomena

Tropical cyclones (called hurricanes, typhoons, or cyclones in different parts of the world) cause serious problems and often destroy everything in their path. They uproot trees, damage buildings, devastate land under cultivation, and cause deaths. The Gulf of Mexico is one of the areas of the planet continually affected by hurricanes. For

CAPRICIOUS FORMS 38-39
THE RAIN ANNOUNCES ITS COMING 40-43
LOST IN THE FOG 44-45
BRIEF FLASH 46-47

WHEN WATER ACCUMULATES 48-49
WATER SCARCITY 50-51
LETHAL FORCE 52-53
DEATH AND DESTRUCTION 54-55

ANATOMY OF A HURRICANE 56-57
WHAT KATRINA TOOK AWAY 58-59
FORESIGHT TO PREVENT TRAGEDIES 60-61

this reason, the government authorities organize preparedness exercises so that the population knows what to do. To understand how hurricanes function and improve forecasts, investigators require detailed information from the heart of the storm. The use of artificial satellites that send clear pictures has contributed greatly to detecting and tracking strong winds, preventing many disasters. ●

Capricious Forms

Clouds are masses of large drops of water and ice crystals. They form because the water vapor contained in the air condenses or freezes as it rises through the troposphere. How the clouds develop depends on the altitude and the velocity of the rising air. Cloud shapes are divided into three basic types: cirrus, cumulus, and stratus. They are also classified as high, medium, and low depending on the altitude they reach above sea level. They are of meteorological interest because they indicate the behavior of the atmosphere. ●

TYPES OF CLOUDS

NAME	MEANING
CIRRUS	FILAMENT
CUMULUS	AGGLOMERATION
STRATUS	BLANKET
NIMBUS	RAIN

Troposphere

The layer closest to the Earth and in which meteorological phenomena occur, including the formation of clouds

Exosphere

300 miles
(500 km)

Mesosphere

50 miles
(90 km)

Stratosphere

30 miles
(50 km)

Troposphere

6 miles
(10 km)

0

HOW THEY ARE FORMED

Clouds are formed when the rising air cools to the point where it cannot hold the water vapor it contains. In such a circumstance, the air is said to be saturated, and the excess water vapor condenses. Cumulonimbus clouds are storm clouds that can reach a height of 43,000 feet (13,000 m) and contain more than 150,000 tons of water.

Convection
The heat of the Sun warms the air near the ground, and because it is less dense than the surrounding air, it rises.

Convergence
When the air coming from one direction meets air from another direction, it is pushed upward.

Geographic elevation
When the air encounters mountains, it is forced to rise. This phenomenon explains why there are often clouds and rain over mountain peaks.

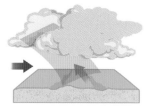

Presence of a front
When two masses of air with different temperatures meet at a front, the warm air rises and clouds are formed.

TROPO

**6 miles
(10 km)**

**-67° F
(-55° C)**
Temperature in the upper part of the troposphere

HIGH CLOUDS

CIRROSTRATUS
A very extensive cloud that eventually covers the whole sky and has the form of a transparent, fibrous-looking veil

**2.5 miles
(4 km)**

**14° F
(-10° C)**
The temperature of the middle part of the troposphere

MEDIUM CLOUDS

CUMULONIMBUS
A storm cloud. It portends intense precipitation in the form of rain, hail, or snow. Its color is white.

CUMULUS
A cloud that is generally dense with well-defined outlines. Cumulus clouds can resemble a mountain of cotton.

**1.2 miles
(2 km)**

**50° F
(10° C)**
Temperature of the lower part of the troposphere

LOW CLOUDS

**59° F
(15° C)**
Temperature at the Earth's surface

0 miles (0 km)

1802
The year that British meteorologist Luke Howard carried out the first scientific study of clouds

P H E R E

CIRRUS
A high, thin cloud with white, delicate filaments composed of ice crystals

CIRROCUMULUS
A cloud formation composed of very small, granulated elements spaced more or less regularly

ALTOCUMULUS
A formation of rounded clouds in groups that can form straight or wavy rows

ALTOSTRATUS
Large, nebulous, compact, uniform, slightly layered masses. Altostratus does not entirely block out the Sun. It is bluish or gray.

STRATOCUMULUS
A cloud that is horizontal and very long. It does not blot out the Sun and is white or gray in color.

NIMBOSTRATUS
Nimbostratus portends more or less continuous precipitation in the form of rain or snow that, in most cases, reaches the ground.

STRATUS
A low cloud that extends over a large area. It can cause drizzle or light snow. Stratus clouds can appear as a gray band along the horizon.

The Inside

The altitude at which clouds are formed depends on the stability of the air and the humidity. The highest and coldest clouds have ice crystals. The lowest and warmest clouds have drops of water. There are also mixed clouds. There are 10 classes of clouds depending on their height above sea level. The highest clouds begin at a height of 2.5 miles (4 km). The mid-level begins at a height of 1.2 to 2.5 miles (2-4 km) and the lowest at 1.2 miles (2 km) high.

1.2 to 5
miles (2-8 km)
Thickness of a storm cloud

150,000
tons of water
can be contained in a storm cloud.

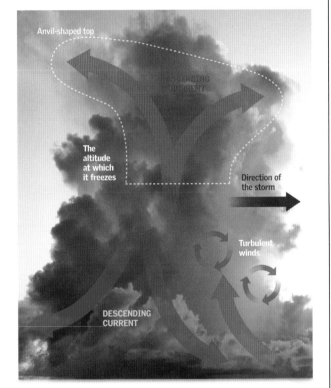

Anvil-shaped top

ASCENDING CURRENT

The altitude at which it freezes

Direction of the storm

Turbulent winds

DESCENDING CURRENT

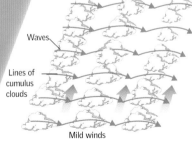

Waves

Lines of cumulus clouds

Mild winds

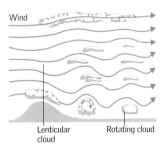

Wind

Lenticular cloud

Rotating cloud

SPECIAL FORMATIONS

CLOUD STREETS
The form of the clouds depends on the winds and the topography of the terrain beneath them. Light winds usually produce lines of cumulus clouds positioned as if along streets. Such waves can be created by differences in surface heating.

LENTICULAR CLOUDS
Mountains usually create waves in the atmosphere on their lee side, and on the crest of each wave lenticular clouds are formed that are held in place by the waves. Rotating clouds are formed by turbulence near the surface.

The Rain Announces Its Coming

The air inside a cloud is in continuous motion. This process causes the drops of water or the crystals of ice that constitute the cloud to collide and join together. In the process, the drops and crystals become too big to be supported by air currents and they fall to the ground as different kinds of precipitation. A drop of rain has a diameter 100 times greater than a droplet in a cloud. The type of precipitation depends on whether the cloud contains drops of water, ice crystals, or both. Depending on the type of cloud and the temperature, the precipitation can be liquid water (rain) or solid (snow or hail). ●

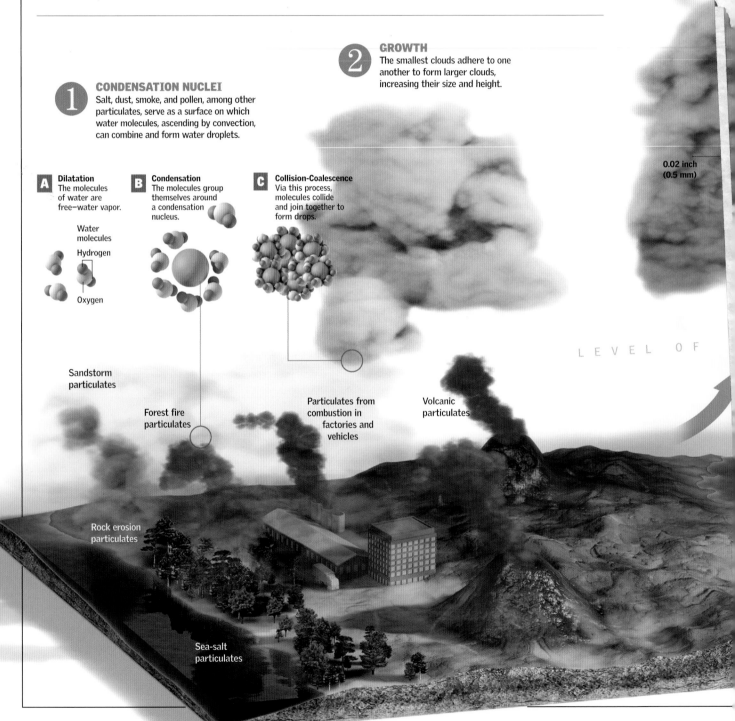

2 GROWTH
The smallest clouds adhere to one another to form larger clouds, increasing their size and height.

1 CONDENSATION NUCLEI
Salt, dust, smoke, and pollen, among other particulates, serve as a surface on which water molecules, ascending by convection, can combine and form water droplets.

A Dilatation
The molecules of water are free—water vapor.

B Condensation
The molecules group themselves around a condensation nucleus.

C Collision-Coalescence
Via this process, molecules collide and join together to form drops.

Water molecules

Hydrogen

Oxygen

0.02 inch
(0.5 mm)

LEVEL OF

Sandstorm particulates

Forest fire particulates

Particulates from combustion in factories and vehicles

Volcanic particulates

Rock erosion particulates

Sea-salt particulates

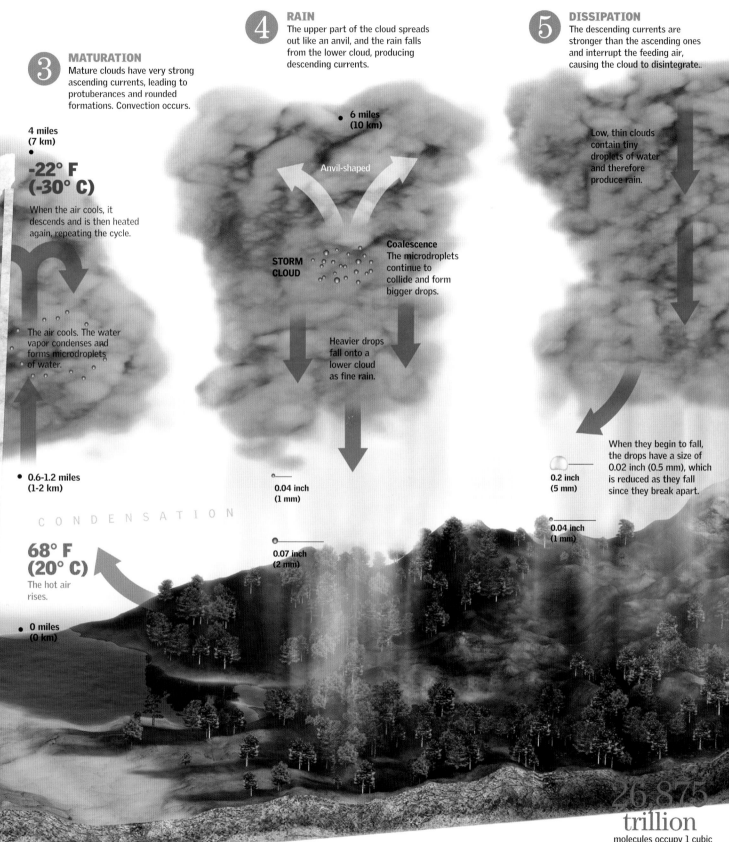

4 **RAIN**
The upper part of the cloud spreads out like an anvil, and the rain falls from the lower cloud, producing descending currents.

5 **DISSIPATION**
The descending currents are stronger than the ascending ones and interrupt the feeding air, causing the cloud to disintegrate..

3 **MATURATION**
Mature clouds have very strong ascending currents, leading to protuberances and rounded formations. Convection occurs.

4 miles
(7 km)

**-22° F
(-30° C)**

When the air cools, it descends and is then heated again, repeating the cycle.

The air cools. The water vapor condenses and forms microdroplets of water.

0.6-1.2 miles
(1-2 km)

6 miles
(10 km)

Anvil-shaped

STORM
CLOUD

Coalescence
The microdroplets continue to collide and form bigger drops.

Heavier drops fall onto a lower cloud as fine rain.

Low, thin clouds contain tiny droplets of water and therefore produce rain.

When they begin to fall, the drops have a size of 0.02 inch (0.5 mm), which is reduced as they fall since they break apart.

0.2 inch
(5 mm)

0.04 inch
(1 mm)

C O N D E N S A T I O N

**68° F
(20° C)**

The hot air rises.

0 miles
(0 km)

0.04 inch
(1 mm)

0.07 inch
(2 mm)

26,875
trillion
molecules occupy 1 cubic millimeter under normal atmospheric conditions.

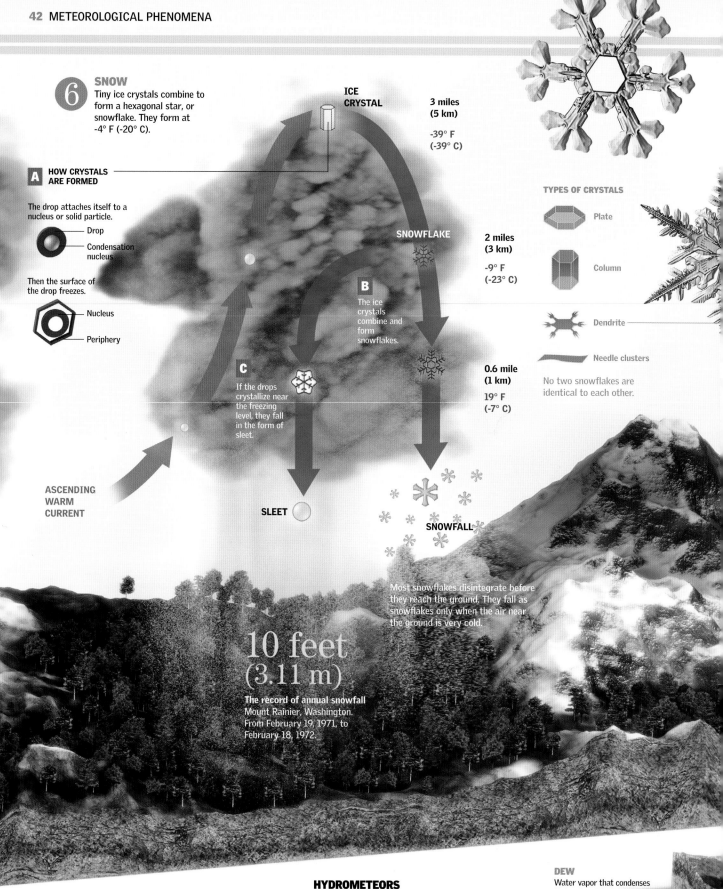

6 SNOW
Tiny ice crystals combine to form a hexagonal star, or snowflake. They form at -4° F (-20° C).

ICE CRYSTAL

3 miles
(5 km)

-39° F
(-39° C)

A HOW CRYSTALS ARE FORMED

The drop attaches itself to a nucleus or solid particle.

- Drop
- Condensation nucleus

Then the surface of the drop freezes.

- Nucleus
- Periphery

SNOWFLAKE

2 miles
(3 km)

-9° F
(-23° C)

B
The ice crystals combine and form snowflakes.

C
If the drops crystallize near the freezing level, they fall in the form of sleet.

0.6 mile
(1 km)

19° F
(-7° C)

ASCENDING WARM CURRENT

SLEET

SNOWFALL

TYPES OF CRYSTALS

- Plate
- Column
- Dendrite
- Needle clusters

No two snowflakes are identical to each other.

Most snowflakes disintegrate before they reach the ground. They fall as snowflakes only when the air near the ground is very cold.

**10 feet
(3.11 m)**

The record of annual snowfall
Mount Rainier, Washington.
From February 19, 1971, to
February 18, 1972.

HYDROMETEORS

Drops of condensed or frozen water in the atmosphere are called hydrometeors. These include rain, fog, hail, mist, snow, and frost.

DEW

Water vapor that condenses during the night into very small drops. The condensation forms on surfaces that radiate heat during the night, such as plants, animals, and buildings.

VARIED FORMS

Snow crystals can have a variety of shapes; most of them have six points, although some have three or 12, and they have hexagonal symmetry in a plane. They can also be cubic crystals, but these form under conditions of extremely low temperature in the highest regions of the troposphere.

Most have **six points**.

The flakes measure between **0.04 and 0.8 inch (1 and 20 mm)**.

B
The droplets freeze, and each time they are carried upward in the cloud, they acquire a new layer of ice. This process, called accretion, increases the size of the hailstone.

Very small hail (0.2 inch [5 mm] or less in diameter) is called snow pellets.

A
Vertical air currents cause the microdroplets to ascend and descend within the cloud.

C
When the hailstones are too heavy to be supported by the ascending air currents, they fall to the ground.

WARM ASCENDING CURRENT

A cloud with a greenish tinge or rain with a whitish color can portend a hailstorm.

7 HAIL
Precipitation in the form of solid lumps of ice. Hail is produced inside storm clouds in which frozen droplets grow in size as they rise and fall within the cloud.

CROSS SECTION OF A HAILSTONE

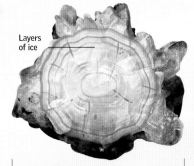

Layers of ice

0.2 to 2 inches (5 to 50 mm)
The typical range of hailstone sizes

2 pounds
(1 kg) **The heaviest hailstones**
that fell on April 14, 1986, in Gopalganj, Bangladesh.

27° F (-3° C)
Temperature of the air

32° F (0° C)
DEW POINT

41° F (5° C)
Temperature of the ground

FROST
Frost forms when the dew point of the air is less than 32° F (0° C), and the water vapor transforms directly into ice when it is deposited on surfaces.

HOAR FROST
Similar to frost but thicker. It usually forms when there is fog.

Lost in the Fog

When atmospheric water vapor condenses near the ground, it forms fog and mist. The fog consists of small droplets of water mixed with smoke and dust particles. Physically the fog is a cloud, but the difference between the two lies in their formation. A cloud develops when the air rises and cools, whereas fog forms when the air is in contact with the ground, which cools it and condenses the water vapor. The atmospheric phenomenon of fog decreases visibility to distances of less than 1 mile (1.6 km) and can affect ground, maritime, and air traffic. When the fog is light, it is called mist. In this case, visibility is reduced to 2 miles (3.2 km). ●

Orographic barrier
Fog develops on lee-side mountain slopes at high altitudes and occurs when the air becomes saturated with moisture.

160 feet
(50 m)

The densest fog affects visibility at this distance and has repercussions on car, boat, and airplane traffic. In many cases, visibility can be zero.

4.
OROGRAPHIC FOG

Dew
The condensation of water vapor on objects that have radiated enough heat to decrease their temperature below the dew point

Fog and Visibility

▶ Visibility is defined as a measure of an observer's ability to recognize objects at a distance through the atmosphere. It is expressed in miles and indicates the visual limit imposed by the presence of fog, mist, dust, smoke, or any type of artificial or natural precipitation in the atmosphere. The different degrees of fog density have various effects on maritime, land, and air traffic.

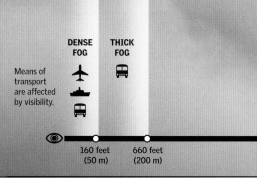

DENSE FOG	THICK FOG	FOG

Means of transport are affected by visibility.

160 feet (50 m)   660 feet (200 m)   0.6 mile (1 km)   1.2 miles (2 km)

Types of Fog

Radiation fog forms during cold nights when the land loses the heat that was absorbed during the day. Frontal fog forms when water that is falling has a higher temperature than the surrounding air; the drops of rain evaporate, and the air tends to become saturated. These fogs are thick and persistent. Advection fog occurs when humid, warm air flows over a surface so cold that it causes the water vapor from the air to condense.

2. FRONTAL FOG
Formed ahead of a warm front

1. RADIATION FOG
This fog appears only on the ground and is caused by radiation cooling of the Earth's surface.

F O G

F O G

3. ADVECTION FOG
Formed when a mass of humid and cool air moves over a surface that is colder than the air

F O G

The air becomes saturated as it ascends.

ASCENDING AIR

Warm air

B L O C K E D F O G

High landmasses

Wind

Mist
Mist consists of salt and other dry particles imperceptible to the naked eye. When the concentration of these particles is very high, the clarity, color, texture, and form of objects we see are diminished.

INVERSION FOG
When a current of warm, humid air flows over the cold water of an ocean or lake, an inversion fog can form. The warm air is cooled by the water, and its moisture condenses into droplets. The warm air traps the cooled air below it, near the surface. High coastal landmasses prevent this type of fog from penetrating very far inland.

6 miles (10 km)
Normal visibility

1.9 miles (3 km)

Brief Flash

Electrical storms are produced in large cumulonimbus-type clouds, which typically bring heavy rains in addition to lightning and thunder. The storms form in areas of low pressure, where the air is warm and less dense than the surrounding atmosphere. Inside the cloud, an enormous electrical charge accumulates, which is then discharged with a zigzag flash between the cloud and the ground, between the cloud and the air, or between one cloud and another. This is how the flash of lightning is unleashed. Moreover, the heat that is released during the discharge generates an expansion and contraction of the air that is called thunder. ●

THUNDER
This is the sound produced by the air when it expands very rapidly, generating shock waves as it is heated.

Cold air
Very hot air
Very hot air
Cold air

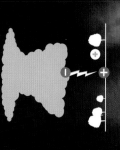

1. ORIGIN
Lightning originates within large cumulonimbus storm clouds. Lightning bolts can have negative or positive electric charges.

Warm air
Cold air

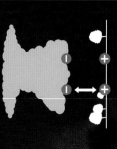

2. INSIDE THE CLOUD
Electrical charges are produced from the collisions between ice or hail crystals. Warm air currents rise, causing the charges in the cloud to shift.

SEPARATION
The charges become separated, with the positive charges accumulating at the top of the cloud and the negative charges at the base.

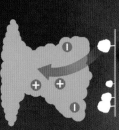

3. ELECTRICAL CHARGES
The cloud's negative charges are attracted to the positive charges of the ground. The difference in electrical potential between the two regions produces the discharge.

INDUCED CHARGE
The negative charge of the base of the cloud induces a positive charge in the ground below it.

4. DISCHARGE
The discharge takes place from the cloud toward the ground after the stepped leader, a channel of ionized air, extends down to the ground.

TYPES OF LIGHTNING
Lightning can be distinguished primarily by the path taken by the electrical charges that cause them.

Cloud-to-air
The electricity moves from the cloud toward an air mass of opposite charge.

Cloud-to-cloud
A lightning flash can occur within a cloud or between two oppositely charged areas.

Cloud-to-ground
Negative charges of the cloud are attracted by the positive charges of the ground.

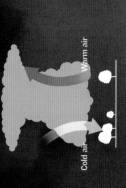

8,700 miles per second
(140,000 km/s) speed

Lightning bolt: 8,700 miles per second (140,000 km/s)

Airplane: 0.2 mile per second (0.3 km/s)

F1 car: 0.06 mile per second (0.1 km/s)

100 million volts
IS THE ELECTRICAL POTENTIAL OF A LIGHTNING BOLT.

A windmill generates 200 volts.

110 volts is consumed by a lamp.

RETURN STROKE In the final phase, the discharge rises from the Earth to the cloud.

DISCHARGE SEQUENCE

channel — 1st phase / 1st return

2nd phase / 2nd return

3rd phase / 3rd return

A The lightning bolt propagates through an ionized channel that branches out to reach the ground. Electrical charges run along the same channel in the opposite direction.

B If the cloud has additional electrical charges, they are propagated to the ground through the channel of the first stroke and generate a second return stroke toward the cloud.

C This discharge, as in the second stroke, does not have branches. When the return discharge ceases, the lightning flash sequence comes to an end.

POINT OF IMPACT

65 feet (20 m)

This is the radius of a lightning bolt's effective range on the surface of the Earth.

LIGHTNING RODS

The primary function of lightning rods is to facilitate the electrostatic discharge, which follows the path of least electrical resistance.

Tip of the conductor

Lightning rod

A lightning rod is an instrument whose purpose is to attract a lightning bolt and channel the electrical discharge to the ground so that it does no harm to buildings or people. A famous experiment by Benjamin Franklin led to the invention of this apparatus. During a lightning storm, he flew a kite into clouds, and it received a strong discharge. That marked the birth of the lightning rod, which consists of an iron rod placed on the highest point of the object to be protected and connected to the ground by a metallic, insulated conductor. The principle of all lightning rods, which terminate in one or more points, is to attract and conduct the lightning bolt to the ground.

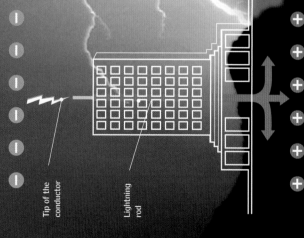

When Water Accumulates

Water is a vital element for life, but in excess it leads to serious consequences for people and their economic activity. Flooding occurs when certain areas that are normally dry are covered with water for a more or less prolonged period. The most important causes are excessive rains, the overflow of rivers and lakes, and giant waves that wash over the coast. Such waves can be the result of unusually high tides caused by strong surface winds or by submarine earthquakes. Walls, dikes, dams, and embankments are used to help prevent flooding. ●

Flooded Land

When land is flooded for days or months, the air in the soil is replaced by water, which prevents the buildup of oxygen, thus affecting the biological activity of plants and the soil itself. In the latter case, if the water does not have sufficient salt, the incomplete decomposition of organic matter and the significant washing away of nutrients make the soil more acidic. If the water contains a great deal of salt, the salt will remain in the soil, causing a different problem: salinization.

Plants with thick, droopy stems

There is so much water on the surface that the soil cannot absorb it.

The soil cannot carry oxygen to the roots.

Reduction

The components of the soil that are oxidized can be reduced and thus change their properties.

Solid particulates

The water causes a decline in oxygen in the aerated spaces of the soil.

Floodplains

Floodplains are areas adjacent to rivers or streams that are subject to recurrent flooding.

Large rivers cross the plains, which suffer from regular flooding

Hydroelectric dam

Flood Control

With the construction of dikes and embankments, the flow of rivers prone to flooding is largely contained.

Agriculture is more productive when water can be controlled.

Channeling water via turbines also generates electricity.

Electrical energy can be made available to houses.

EMBANKMENT
Earthen embankments help contain rivers that tend to overflow and temporarily change course.

STORM DIKES
In areas where the coast is low and exposed to flooding, protective dikes have been constructed against high tides and powerful waves.

Torrential Rains

Caused by low pressure systems, instability of the air mass, and high humidity

Torrential rains raise the level of the water in the rivers and the riverbeds.

Snow increases runoff into the rivers.

Little or no rain penetrates into the valley slopes covered with pines.

Principal river

Tributary river

Low-lying terrain
The main river cannot contain the increased flow of the tributary rivers.

Houses and trees covered with water

Natural course of the river

250,000
Victims of flooding in the Bay of Bengal, Bangladesh, in 1970

Transformers
Their job is to transform the voltage of the electric current.

Dam
stores water to divert it or to regulate its flow outside the riverbed.

Filtering grates
prevent the passage of unwanted objects in the water used to produce hydroelectric power.

Hydroelectric Plants

use the force and velocity of running water to turn turbines. There are two types: run-off-river (which uses the natural kinetic energy of the river's running waters) and reservoir (where the water accumulates behind dams and is then released under increased pressure to the power plant).

Electrical power lines

Elevation of the reservoir

Electrical generator
Equipment that produces electricity by converting the mechanical energy of the rotating turbine into electrical energy

Water Scarcity

I n deserts, drought from lack of rain is customary, but in arid, semiarid, and subhumid regions, desertification occurs when for weeks, months, or years the land is degraded because of climatic variations. A high-pressure center that stays in a certain location longer than usual can be the cause of this phenomenon. Soils are able to put up with a certain dry period, but when the water table decreases drastically, the drought can turn into a natural catastrophe. ●

CYCLONIC CURRENT

A RAIN
Caused by cyclonic (low pressure) air currents.

1

SATURATED SOIL
The water that falls as precipitation may be more than the soil can absorb, and it descends toward aquifers.

Solid particulates

Remaining water

2

METEOROLOGICAL DROUGHT
The condition that results when precipitation is much lower than normal levels for that location. It is generally determined based on comparison with average rainfall.

THE DRIEST ZONES
coincide with deserts. For example, in the Atacama Desert in northern Chile, not a single drop of water fell between 1903 and 1917.

100 years
The region of the Sahel has endured periods of devastating droughts lasting this long.

KEY
● Areas of insufficient rain for normal vegetation and harvests

1933-37 ——— UNITED
The Dust Bowl STATES
was created.
1962-66
Affected the states
of the Northeast
1977
Water is rationed in
California.

1975-76
Less than 50% of
the average rainfall

ENGLAND

1965-67
1.5 million deaths
caused by
INDIA —— drought

SAHEL

1967-69
Numerous
forest fires AUSTRALIA

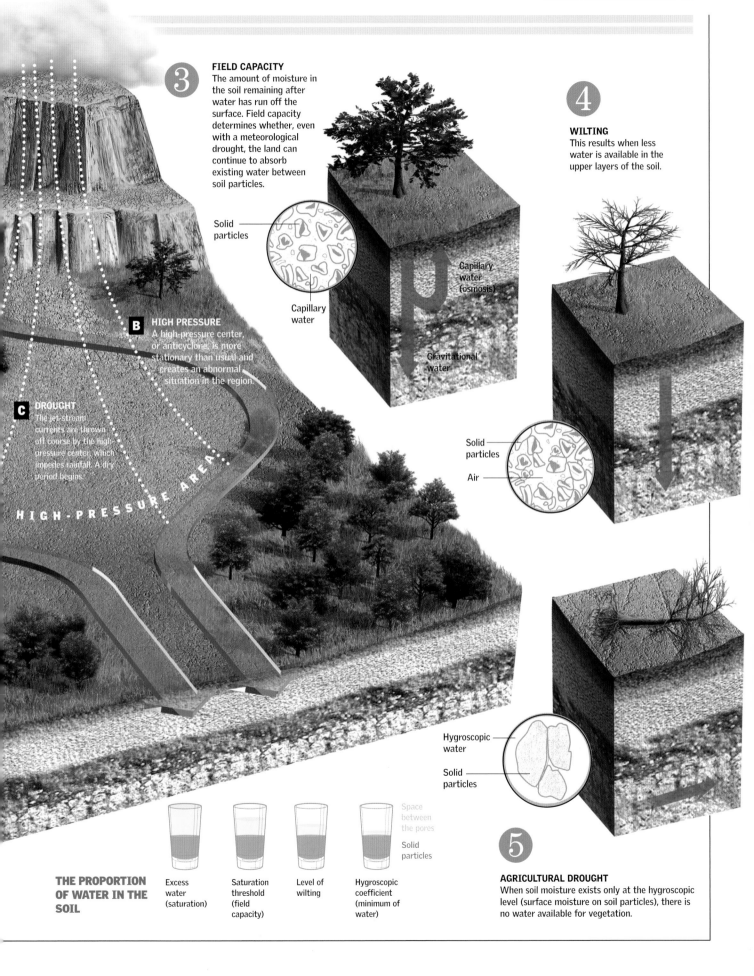

3 **FIELD CAPACITY**
The amount of moisture in the soil remaining after water has run off the surface. Field capacity determines whether, even with a meteorological drought, the land can continue to absorb existing water between soil particles.

4 **WILTING**
This results when less water is available in the upper layers of the soil.

B **HIGH PRESSURE**
A high-pressure center, or anticyclone, is more stationary than usual and creates an abnormal situation in the region.

C **DROUGHT**
The jet-stream currents are thrown off course by the high-pressure center, which impedes rainfall. A dry period begins.

HIGH-PRESSURE AREA

Solid particles

Capillary water

Capillary water (osmosis)

Gravitational water

Solid particles

Air

Hygroscopic water

Solid particles

THE PROPORTION OF WATER IN THE SOIL

Excess water (saturation)

Saturation threshold (field capacity)

Level of wilting

Hygroscopic coefficient (minimum of water)

Space between the pores

Solid particles

5 **AGRICULTURAL DROUGHT**
When soil moisture exists only at the hygroscopic level (surface moisture on soil particles), there is no water available for vegetation.

Lethal Force

ornadoes are the most violent storms of nature. They are generated by electrical storms (or sometimes as the result of a hurricane), and they take the form of powerful funnel-shaped whirlwinds that extend from the sky to the ground. In these storms, moving air is mixed with soil and other matter rotating at velocities as high as 300 miles per hour (480 km/h). They can uproot trees, destroy buildings, and turn harmless objects into deadly airborne projectiles. A tornado can devastate a whole neighborhood within seconds.

How They Form

➤ Tornadoes begin to form when a current of warm air ascends inside a cumulonimbus cloud and begins to rotate under the influence of winds in the upper part of the cloud. From the base of the column, air is sucked toward the inside of the turning spiral. The air

rotates faster as it approaches the center of the column. This increases the force of the ascending current, and the column continues to grow until it stretches from high in the clouds to the ground. Because of their short duration, they are difficult to study and predict.

1.

BEGINNING OF A TORNADO
When the winds meet, they cause the air to rotate in a clockwise direction in the Southern Hemisphere and in the reverse direction in the Northern Hemisphere.

Strong wind

Mild Wind

Spinning funnel of air

2.

ROTATION
The circulation of the air causes a decrease in pressure at the center of the storm, creating a central column of air.

Convection

6 miles (10 km)

Maximum height that it can attain

Maximum diameter

0.6 mile (1 km)

TOP
The top of the tornado remains inside the cloud.

300 miles per hour (480 km/h)

Maximum velocity the tornado winds can attain

VORTEX
Column of air that forms the lower part of a tornado; a funnel that generates violent winds and draws in air. It usually acquires the dark color of the dust it sucks up from the ground, but it can be invisible.

MULTIPLE VORTICES
Some tornadoes have a number of vortices.

Where and When

Most tornadoes occur in agricultural areas. The humidity and heat of the spring and summer are required to feed the storms that produce them. In order to grow, crops require both the humidity and temperature variations associated with the seasons.

● Tornadoes
● Agricultural areas

3:00 P.M.–9:00 P.M.
The period of the day with the highest probability of tornado formation

1,000
tornadoes are generated on average annually in the United States.

125 miles (200 km)
The length of the path along the ground over which a tornado can move

Some tornadoes are so powerful that they can rip the roofs off houses.

The tornado generally moves from the southwest to the northeast.

SPIRALING WINDS
First a cloud funnel appears that can then extend to touch the ground.

3.

DESCENT
The central whirling column continues to descend within the cloud, perforating it in the direction of the ground.

Cumulonimbus

Warm and humid wind

Cold and dry wind

Storm

Humid wind

4.

THE OUTCOME
The tornado reaches the Earth and depending on its intensity can send the roofs of buildings flying.

PATH
Normally the tornado path is no more than 160 to 330 feet (50–100 m) wide.

FUJITA SCALE
The Fujita-Pearson scale was created by Theodore Fujita to classify tornadoes according to the damage caused by the wind force to

WIND VELOCITY MILES PER HOUR (KM/H)	40-72 (64-116)	73-112 (117-180)	113-157 (181-253)	158-206 (254-332)	207-260 (333-418)	261-320 (420-512)
CATEGORY	F0	F1	F2	F3	F4	F5
EFFECTS	Damage to chimneys, tree	Mobile homes ripped from their	Mobile homes destroyed, trees	Roofs and walls demolished, cars and	Solidly built walls blown	Houses uprooted from their foundations and

Death and Destruction

O f the 1,000 tornadoes that annually strike the United States, there is one that has the unfortunate distinction of being one of the worst: the Tri-State tornado, which occurred on March 18, 1925, and caused extreme devastation. It moved across Missouri, Illinois, and Indiana, destroying homes and causing the confirmed deaths of 695 people, although it is believed that the number may have been much higher. The tornado traveled 230 miles (368 km) at an average velocity of 66 miles an hour (105 km/h), and its duration set a record at three hours and 30 minutes. It has been rated on the Fujita scale as an F5 tornado—one of the most damaging—and caused losses to the United States of $17 million. ●

MISSOURI (U.S.)
Latitude 37° N
Longitude 93° W

Value on the Fujita scale	**F5**
Duration	**3 hours 30 minutes**
Average velocity	**66 miles per hour (105 km/h)**

1:01 P.M.
First contact with the ground

ELLINGTON
First town affected
One dead

71 miles per hour (115 km/h)

REDFORD
Town hit by tornado

ANNAPOLIS AND LEADANNA
Large number of victims
75 injured and 2 dead

66 miles per hour (107 km/h)

90 percent destroyed

BIEHLE
A number of houses destroyed

60 miles per hour (96 km/h)

100 percent destroyed

30 percent destroyed

DE SOTO
Partial destruction but a large number of victims
69 dead

GORHAM
Town in ruins
34 dead

MURPHYSBORO
Town with the greatest number of fatalities
234 dead

40 percent destroyed

M I S S O U R I

4:30 P.M.
Final contact with the ground

230 miles (368 km)
TOTAL PATH TRAVELLED

38 miles
(60.5 km)

9° of rotation

190 miles (307.5 km)

70 miles per hour
(115 km/h)
Velocity

65 miles per hour
(104 km/h)
Average velocity

71 miles per hour
(115 km/h)

OWENSVILLE
Serious damage
to houses

I N D I A N A

PARRISH
Almost total
destruction
22 dead

**90
percent**
destroyed

Rural area

60 miles per hour
(96 km/h)

GRIFFIN
150 houses
destroyed, and
many children
killed.

**100
percent**
destroyed

PRINCETON
Half of the town
destroyed
65 deaths

**50
percent**
destroyed

55 miles per hour
(90 km/h)

In **40 minutes,
541 people died.**

WEST FRANKFORT
Partial destruction
**450 wounded
and 127 dead**

**20
percent**
destroyed

Tornadoes in the United States

Unlike hurricanes, which are tropical storms primarily affecting the
Gulf of Mexico, tornadoes are phenomena that occur between the
Great Plains of the United States, the Rocky Mountains, and the Gulf of
Mexico and usually appear in the spring and summer.

**3:00 P.M.
-9:00 P.M.**
The period of the day
with the highest
probability of tornado
formation

1,000
The number of
tornadoes occurring
per year in the
United States

South
Dakota

Indiana

Arkansas
Alabama
Georgia

Texas
Louisiana

Florida

Gulf of
Mexico

I L L I N O I S

**THE TOWN OF
GRIFFIN, IN
THE STATE OF
INDIANA, WAS
LEFT IN RUINS.**

15,000
houses destroyed

17 million
dollars in losses

THE 10 MOST DEVASTATING TORNADOES

Victims

- Deaths
- Injuries

	Tri-State 1925	Natchez 1840	St. Louis 1896	Tupelo 1936	Gainesville 1936	Woodward 1947	Amite/Pine/Purvis 1908	New Richmond 1889	Flint 1953	Waco 1953
Injuries	2,027	109	1,000	700	1,600	970	770	200	844	597
Deaths	695	317	255	216	203	181	143	117	115	114

Anatomy of a Hurricane

A hurricane, with its ferocious winds, banks of clouds, and torrential rains, is the most spectacular meteorological phenomenon of the Earth's weather. It is characterized by an intense low-pressure center surrounded by cloud bands arranged in spiral form; these rotate around the eye of the hurricane in a clockwise direction in the Southern Hemisphere and in the opposite direction in the Northern Hemisphere. While tornadoes are brief and relatively limited, hurricanes are enormous and slow-moving, and their passage usually takes many lives. ●

DAY 1
A jumble of clouds is formed.

1.

BIRTH
Forms over warm seas, aided by winds in opposing directions, high temperatures, humidity, and the rotation of the Earth

NH
SH
Hurricanes in the Northern Hemisphere rotate counterclockwise, and those in the Southern Hemisphere rotate clockwise.

FRINGES OF STORM CLOUDS
otate violently around the central zone.

THE EYE
Central area, has very low pressure

Descending air currents

The air wraps around the eye.

Cloud bands in the form of a spiral

EYE WALL
The strongest winds are formed.

VAPOR
Rises warm from the sea, forming a column of clouds. It rises 3,900 feet (1,200 m) in the center of the storm.

Strong ascendant currents

80° F
(27° C)
is the minimum temperature that water on the surface of the ocean will evaporate at.

The trade winds are pulled toward the storm.

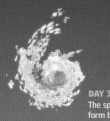

DAY 2
The clouds begin to rotate.

DAY 3
The spiral form becomes more defined.

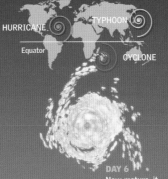

DAY 6
Now mature, it displays a visible eye.

HURRICANE   TYPHOON

Equator

CYCLONE

DANGER ZONE

The areas that are vulnerable to hurricanes in the United States include the Atlantic coast and the coast along the Gulf of Mexico, from Texas to Maine. The Caribbean and the tropical areas of the western Pacific, including Hawaii, Guam, American Samoa, and Saipan, are also zones frequented by hurricanes.

DAY 12
The hurricane begins to break apart when it makes landfall.

2. **DEVELOPMENT**

Begins to ascend, twisting in a spiral around a low-pressure zone

19 miles per hour
(30 km/h)

VELOCITY AT WHICH IT APPROACHES THE COAST

FRICTION
When the hurricane reaches the mainland, it moves more slowly; it is very destructive in this stage, since it is here that populated cities are located.

3. **DEATH**

As they pass from the sea to the land, they cause enormous damage. Hurricanes gradually dissipate over land from the lack of water vapor.

The high-altitude winds blow from outside the storm.

PATH OF THE HURRICANE

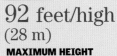

92 feet/high
(28 m)

MAXIMUM HEIGHT REACHED BY THE WAVES

1
2
3
4
5

WIND ACTIVITY

Light winds give it direction and permit it to grow.

The winds flow outward.

CLASSIFICATION OF DAMAGE DONE
Saffir-Simpson category

	Damage	Speed miles per hour (km/h)	High Tide feet (m)
CLASS 1	minimum	74 to 95 (119 to 153)	4 to 5 (1.2 to 1.5)
CLASS 2	moderate	96 to 110 (154 to 177)	6 to 8 (1.8 to 2.4)
CLASS 3	extensive	111 to 130 (178 to 209)	9 to 12 (2.7 to 3.6)
CLASS 4	extreme	131 to 155 (210 to 250)	13 to 18 (3.9 to 5.4)
CLASS 5	catastrophic	more than 155 (250)	more than 18 (5.4)

What Katrina Took Away

Hurricane Katrina lashed the south and the center of the United States in August 2005. The force of the wind razed thousands of houses, buildings, oil installations, highways, and bridges, leaving a vast area of the country without communication and some heavily populated areas without provisions. It resulted in extensive material damage and thousands of deaths in Florida, the Bahamas, Louisiana, and Mississippi. Satellite images reveal the scope of the disaster, considered one of the most devastating in the history of the country. ●

THE WATER advances toward the city, invading the central regions.

LAKE PONTCHARTRAIN

DIKES were breached by the water and the wind, causing a great flood.

6:00 A.M. The time when the hurricane made landfall

17TH STREET CANAL

ORLEANS AVENUE CANAL

LONDON AVENUE CANAL

80% Area of New Orleans affected by flooding

Area most affected by the flood

Areas most affected by the flood

OVER 1,500 Deaths confirmed after Katrina

75% of the inhabitants of this zone were evacuated.

OVER 75 billion dollars was the cost of the repairs.

The hurricane winds pushed the water 14 feet (4.3 m) above the normal sea level.

Along with the storm, the backed-up water reaches the dikes of the Mississippi River.

THE WINDS
At 155 miles per hour (250 km/h), they force the water against the protective walls..

NEW ORLEANS

Latitude 30° N

Longitude 90° W

Area	**360 square miles (933 square kilometers)**
Number of inhabitants	**500,000**
Altitude (above sea level)	**10 feet (3 m)**

Lousiana

New Orleans

14   Huracanes fueron registrados en 2005.

26   El total de tormentas tropicales registradas en el año 2005.

AUGUST 23
A tropical depression forms in the Bahamas. It intensifies and becomes tropical storm Katrina. On August 25, it makes landfall in Florida as a category 1 hurricane.

AUGUST 27
Leaves the Gulf of Mexico and reaches category 3. On August 28, it is transformed from category 3 to category 5 and increases in size.

CATEGORY 5   CATEGORY 3

AUGUST 29
In the early hours, it makes landfall in Louisiana as a category 4 hurricane. A little later, it makes landfall for the third time, in Mississippi.

CATEGORY 4

155 miles per hour
(250 km/h)
MAXIMUM WIND SPEED

SEPTEMBER 1
What remains of the hurricane is weakened as it moves north to Canada, where it dissipates.

Direction of the hurricane

Foresight to Prevent Tragedies

Hurricanes usually lash specific regions of the planet, and the population must become aware of the disasters that can strike the community. Each family must know which area of the house is the most secure in case the roof, a door, or a window collapses. They must also know when it is time to go to a shelter or if it is better to remain at home. Another important precaution is to organize and store all family documents and real-estate records in a water- and fireproof strongbox. ●

BEFORE THE HURRICANE
If you live in a hurricane-prone area, it is recommended that you know the emergency plans of the community and that you have a plan of action for your family.

Secure all the doors and windows to keep them from opening.

Store nonperishable food and potable water.

Reinforce roof tiles to keep them from being loosened.

Keep valuable objects and documents in a waterproof container.

Follow news reports with a battery-powered radio.

Keep the car supplied with a full tank of fuel just in case.

Administer first aid when necessary.

HOW TO PREPARE EMERGENCY EQUIPMENT
A complete first-aid kit must be prepared and available. Consult a pharmacist or your family physician.

HOW TO PREPARE DOCUMENTATION
To be prepared for evacuation, keep family documents in good order.

First-aid kit
Check the first-aid kit and replace any expired items.

Inventory
Make a complete list of belongings of each person.

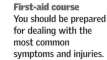
First-aid course
You should be prepared for dealing with the most common symptoms and injuries.

Personal ID
It is important for everyone to have an ID card.

③ AFTER THE HURRICANE

First verify that everyone in the family is well and that there are no injuries. Do not touch loose cables or fallen poles. Call the fire department or the police in case you need food, clothing, or immediate medication.

② DURING THE HURRICANE

The important thing is to remain calm and to stay informed via radio or television about the path of the hurricane. Move away from doors and windows. Do not leave until the authorities announce the danger from the hurricane has ended.

Help people who are injured or trapped.

Keep documents confirming your ownership of property close at hand.

Return home only when the authorities say that it is safe.

Do not drink water unless you are sure it is potable.

Use the telephone only for emergency calls.

Verify that there are no natural-gas leaks or damage to the electrical system.

Disconnect all electrical devices and shut off the house circuit breaker.

Use a battery-powered radio to tune into local stations to get information.

Check the most fire-prone areas.

Do not touch wires or damaged electrical equipment.

Turn off the main water valve and the main gas valve.

When you are on the move, use caution whether on foot or driving.

Meteorology

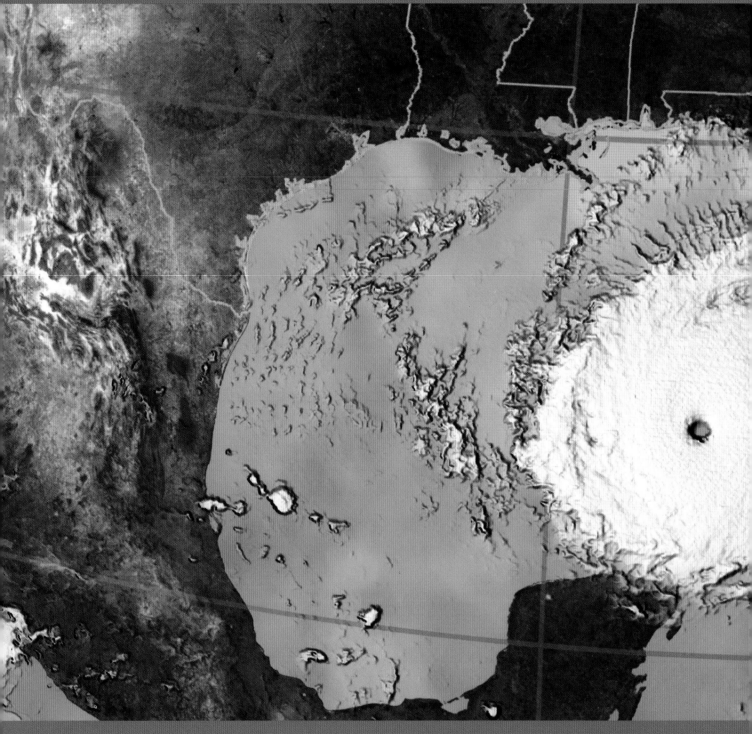

The use of satellites orbiting the Earth, recording the coming of rain, air currents, and clouds, allows us to know with some hours of advance warning if a severe storm is heading toward a certain point on the planet. Counting on this type of precise information about when and where tropical cyclones will occur, for example, has allowed government

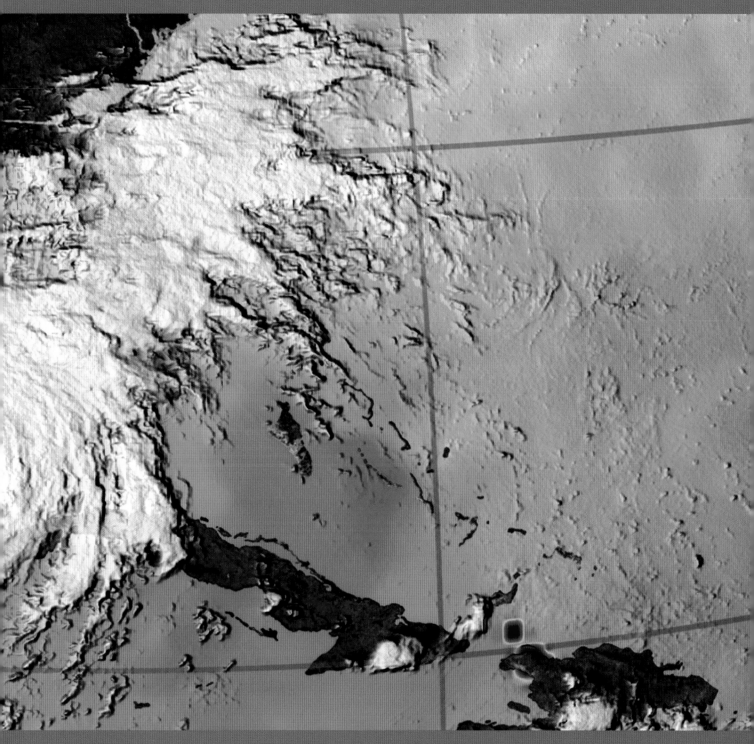

WEATHER FOLKLORE 64-65
COMPILATION OF INFORMATION 66-67
INSTANTANEOUS MAPS 68-69
RAIN, COLD, OR HEAT 70-71
MOBILE SATELLITES 72-73

RITA, SEPTEMBER 2003
The image from the GOES-12 satellite shows the configuration of Hurricane Rita in the eastern portion of the Gulf of Mexico.

officials to coordinate the evacuation of people from the affected zones. The surface of the planet is also monitored by a system of meteorological stations placed hundreds of miles from each other. These collect information from and send information to all areas of the world so that meteorologists can prepare maps, graphics, and predictions to inform the public. ●

Weather Folklore

Before the development of meteorology as we know it today, people observed in nature signs that allowed them to predict rains, floods, or strong winds. All this knowledge has been transmitted over the centuries in the form of proverbs or rhymes. Most of these fragments of meteorological knowledge lack a scientific foundation, but some of them reflect certain principles. Plants and animals play a major role in these observations. ●

Signs from Plants and Animals

In every rural community, concern for the harvest and dependency on weather resulted in a series of beliefs, with varying degrees of accuracy, taken as prophesies of later events. In any case, even though it is certain that people as well as plants and animals react to the current weather, there is nothing to indicate that this might reveal anything about the weather in the future except to the degree that an incipient change is related to the current weather. For example, some signs accompany the increase in humidity that occurs prior to the passage of a cold front.

Swallow

When swallows fly low, get your rain gear in tow.
Swallows usually appear before a heavy rain.

OPEN AND CLOSED PINECONES
Open pinecones mean dry weather; closed pinecones mean humid weather.

DRY SEAWEED
The lower the humidity, the more probable it is that the next day will be dry.

Donkey

I hear donkeys braying; I am sure it will rain today.
The animals react to the existing weather. It is a sign associated with the increased humidity in the environment.

Toad

When you see a toad walking, it will be a wet spring.
When a toad is swimming in the water, this means it will soon rain. If it stays in the water without moving, the rain will last for some time.

Moon

When the Moon has a halo, tomorrow will have wet or bad weather.
Halos occur as a consequence of the refraction of light by ice crystals in cirrostratus clouds covering the Sun or Moon. They portend a warm front, which will be followed by rain.

Almanac Forecasts

In the 16th century, almanacs with weather forecasts were sold throughout Europe. Each month of the year has its own refrain, although this depends on the hemisphere a person lives in. The monthly and annual calendars offered agricultural and medical advice. From the most remote times, there was a general belief that the Moon determined the behavior of the atmosphere and that variations in the weather were caused by changes in the phase of the Moon. Some examples of these popular sayings are: "Sweet April showers do spring May flowers;" "After a dark winter's night, the next day will be bright."

Clouds

Clouds with a fringe or lining— secure your sails well.
This relates to clouds that are carried by winds at high altitudes; these clouds are often a sign that a low-pressure system, or cyclone, is approaching.

WEATHER PREDICTION
There are thousands of refrains that refer to changes in weather conditions. Here are some examples.

WIND
Wind from the east, rain like a beast.

MORNING DEW
Dew and cool in May, bring wine to the vine and hay to the cow.

CLEAR SUNSET
Rainbow at sundown, good weather at dawn.

OAK
If the leaves of the oak fall before those of the ash, the summer will be dry.

ASH
If the leaves of the ash fall before those of the oak, the summer will be wet.

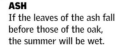

Snails

When you see a black slug in your way, rain is not far away.
Snails are usually hidden in the garden. You see them only on humid days, just prior to the rain.

Compilation of Information

Most of the information available regarding climatic data comes from the record that meteorologists everywhere in the world keep regarding cloud cover, temperature, the force and direction of the wind, air pressure, visibility, and precipitation. Then from each meteorological station, the data is sent by radio or satellite, and this makes it possible to make forecasts and maps. ●

Radar

ANEROID BAROMETER
measures atmospheric pressure. Changes are shown by the pointers.

Scale
Spring

Spiral spring

Metal drum

Levers   Chains

Atmospheric pressure

Vacuum
760 mm

Mercury

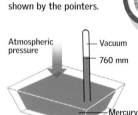

MERCURY BAROMETER
An instrument used to measure atmospheric pressure. It consists of a glass tube full of mercury, with the open end submerged in a reservoir.

BAROGRAPH
measures the atmospheric pressure and records its changes over time.

Workplace

▶ A typical meteorological station checks the temperature, humidity, wind velocity and direction, solar radiation, rain, and barometric pressure. In some places, soil temperature and flow of nearby rivers are also monitored. The compilation of this data makes it possible to predict different meteorological phenomena.

The light strikes and is concentrated as it traverses the sphere.

HELIOPHANOGRAPH
An instrument used to measure the number of hours of sunlight. It consists of a glass sphere that acts as a lens to concentrate sunlight. The light is projected onto a piece of cardboard behind the sphere. The cardboard is burned according to the intensity of the light.

IMPRESSION
The concentrated rays of sunlight burn cardboard placed behind the glass sphere.

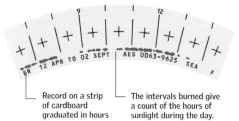

9
12
GR   12 APR TO 02 SEPT   AES 0063-9625   SEA   F

Record on a strip of cardboard graduated in hours

The intervals burned give a count of the hours of sunlight during the day.

EVAPORIMETER
As its name indicates, it measures the effective evaporation of water from a mass of liquid in the open air, from its loss from the surface through transformation to water vapor.

WEATHER VANE
shows which way the wind is blowing. It is a perfectly balanced mechanical system.

Indicates the direction of the wind

Three equally spaced cups record the intensity of the wind.

DATA RECORDER
records the data obtained.

ANEMOMETER
measures the speed of the wind. This instrument is activated by the wind, which turns three hemispherical cups mounted on a vertical rod firmly placed in the ground.

MAXIMUM THERMOMETER
shows the highest temperature of the day. The capillary with mercury is calibrated in the bulb.

Bulb with mercury

Bulb with alcohol

2 °

MINIMUM THERMOMETER
indicates the lowest temperature of the day. It has a fork-shaped bulb.

HYGROTHERMOGRAPH
simultaneously records the air temperature and relative humidity. A thermograph and a hygrograph independently make records on paper of the daily variations in temperature and humidity.

METEOROLOGICAL SHELTER
It is built of wood or fiberglass on a base that insulates it from the soil and protects certain instruments (thermometers, psychrometers, and others) from solar radiation. Screens in the windows ensure good ventilation.

Double circulation of the air to prevent the heating of the instruments when the radiation is very intense

Psychrometer

Maximum and minimum thermometers

Hygrothermograph

Slats allow the air to flow through freely without creating currents.

PSYCHROMETER
measures the relative humidity of the air. It consists of two thermometers and two bulbs (one dry and one covered with muslin that is always kept damp).

Dry-bulb thermometer

Wet-bulb thermometer

Container of distilled water

Weather vane

Anemometer

Data recorder

Solar panel

Control unit

Weather Station

Meteorologists collect data at different heights. They use various instruments at ground level: a thermometer for temperature, a hygrometer for humidity, and a barometer for atmospheric pressure.

In the Northern Hemisphere, the doors should be oriented toward the north to prevent the Sun's rays from striking the instruments when observations are being made.

Thermometer

Mouth

Drum

Recording pen

Siphon

Collector container

Wooden platform

RAIN METER
This is used to keep a chronological record of the amount of water falling as rain.

RAIN GAUGE
The precipitation that falls on the ground in the form of rain is collected by the rain gauge.

Rain Meter

Automatic Weather Station

An automatic meteorological station uses electrical sensors to record temperature, humidity, wind velocity and direction, atmospheric pressure, and rainfall, among other parameters. The readings are processed by microprocessors and transmitted via an automatic system. This station functions autonomously, 24 hours a day, powered by solar energy (solar panels) or wind energy.

Instantaneous Maps

W eather maps represent at any given moment the state of the atmosphere at different altitudes. These maps are made based on the information provided by meteorological stations and are useful for specialists. The data collected by them include various values for pressure and temperature that make it possible to forecast the probability of precipitation, whether the weather will remain stable, or if it will change because a weather front is moving in. ●

NOMENCLATURE

Every meteorological map carries a label that indicates the date and time it was made.

12 indicates the hour and Z Greenwich Mean Time.

This map is prepared with the initial values of Tuesday, September 2.

It indicates the initial values.

1686

is the year in which English astronomer Edmond Halley made the first meteorological map.

SYMBOLS

There are a number of different symbols to represent different kinds of fronts.

WARM A warm air mass with local storms is advancing.

COLD A cold air mass with rain is advancing.

STATIONARY Moderately bad weather and little change of temperature

OCCLUDED FRONT
It is mixed; it will act first as a warm front and then as a cold front.

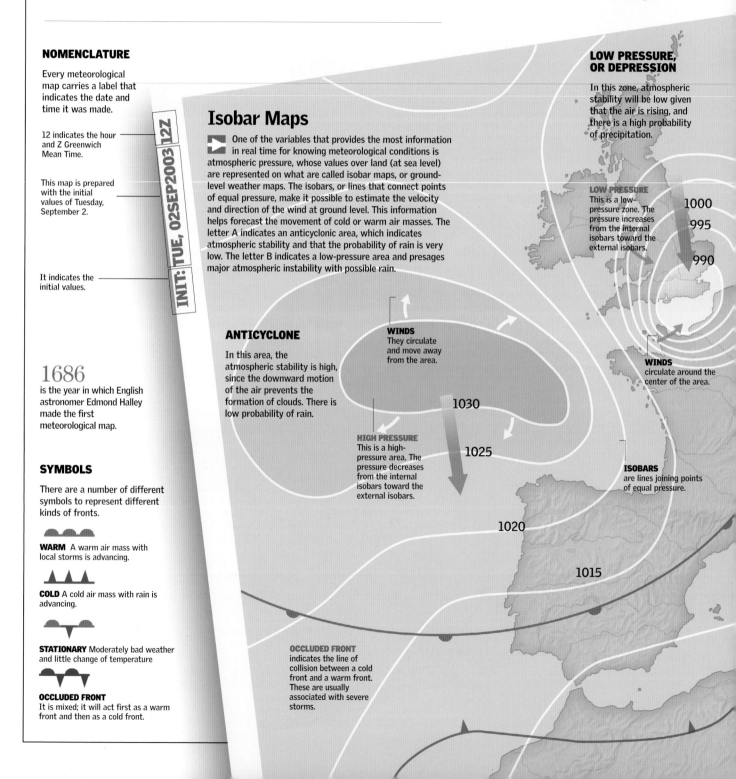

INIT: TUE, 02SEP2003 12Z

Isobar Maps

One of the variables that provides the most information in real time for knowing meteorological conditions is atmospheric pressure, whose values over land (at sea level) are represented on what are called isobar maps, or ground-level weather maps. The isobars, or lines that connect points of equal pressure, make it possible to estimate the velocity and direction of the wind at ground level. This information helps forecast the movement of cold or warm air masses. The letter A indicates an anticyclonic area, which indicates atmospheric stability and that the probability of rain is very low. The letter B indicates a low-pressure area and presages major atmospheric instability with possible rain.

ANTICYCLONE

In this area, the atmospheric stability is high, since the downward motion of the air prevents the formation of clouds. There is low probability of rain.

WINDS
They circulate and move away from the area.

HIGH PRESSURE
This is a high-pressure area. The pressure decreases from the internal isobars toward the external isobars.

LOW PRESSURE, OR DEPRESSION

In this zone, atmospheric stability will be low given that the air is rising, and there is a high probability of precipitation.

LOW PRESSURE
This is a low-pressure zone. The pressure increases from the internal isobars toward the external isobars.

WINDS
circulate around the center of the area.

ISOBARS
are lines joining points of equal pressure.

OCCLUDED FRONT
indicates the line of collision between a cold front and a warm front. These are usually associated with severe storms.

1000
995
990
1030
1025
1020
1015

Upper-air Map

▶ Another type of map, which is used to analyze upper-air weather conditions, is an upper-level, or geopotential, map. On these maps, contour lines connect points located at the same altitude for a certain pressure level (normally 500 hectopascals [hPa]) and correlate with the temperature of the air in the higher layers of the troposphere (at 16,400 feet [5,000 meters] altitude on the 500 hPa map). The temperature is represented in each region of the troposphere by lines called isotherms.

WINDS

The direction and intensity of the winds are indicated by a segment with a circle at its end, which indicates the direction from which the wind is blowing. On this segment, perpendicular lines are traced that indicate the velocity of the wind in knots, where one knot equals 1.2 miles per hour (1.9 km/h).

SYMBOLS
The direction of the wind is represented by these symbols:

POSITION
The line indicates the direction of the wind. It can be north, northeast, east, southeast, south, southwest, west, or northwest.

BAD WEATHER
Instability and high probability of abundant rain

LOW-PRESSURE TROUGH

This phenomenon increases the probability of bad weather. A low-pressure trough has a low geopotential value.

HIGH-PRESSURE RIDGE

Area of high geopotential values in which the chances of rain are slight

GOOD WEATHER
Atmospheric stability and low expectation of precipitation

OVERCAST SKY
A black circle indicates an overcast sky and a white circle a clear sky.

WIND VELOCITY
A short line indicates five knots, a longer line indicates 10 knots, and a terminal triangle indicates more than 40 knots.

LOW-PRESSURE TROUGH AXIS

HIGH-PRESSURE RIDGE AXIS

UPPER-LEVEL MAPS

The contour lines traced in these charts connect points of equal geopotential height which define high-pressure ridges and low-pressure troughs. The wind direction is parallel to these lines. These charts are used to prepare weather forecasts.

250 hPa	36,100 FEET (11,000 METERS)
500 hPa	18,000 FEET (5,500 METERS)
700 hPa	9,800 FEET (3,000 METERS)
850 hPa	4,900 FEET (1,500 METERS)
SURFACE	0 FEET (0 METERS)

500 HPA
The first pressure value that represents a geopotential of 500 hectopascals (hPa)

600 596 592 588 584 580 576 572 568 564 560 556 552 548 544 540 536 532 528 524 520 516 512 508 504 500 496 492 488 484 480 476

Rain, Cold, or Heat

Knowing ahead of time what the weather will be is sometimes a question of life or death. The damage resulting from a torrential rain or a heavy snowfall can be avoided thanks to the forecasts of meteorologists. The forecasts they make are based on information gathered from many sources, including instruments on the ground, in the air, and at sea. Despite the use of sophisticated information systems, the weather can be forecast only for the next few hours or days. Nonetheless, it is very useful in helping to prevent major catastrophes. ●

DATA COLLECTION

The World Meteorological Organization acts as a center for receiving and transmitting data coming from various stations located in the air, on the ocean, and on land.

On Land

The observations made at ground level are more numerous than those made at higher altitudes. They include measurements of atmospheric pressure, temperature, humidity, wind direction and velocity, the extent and altitude of cloud cover, visibility, and precipitation.

METEOROLOGICAL STATION

Measurements at ground level permit the collection of partial data. Thermometers measure temperature, the hygrometer measures humidity, and the barometer measures atmospheric pressure.

In the Air

Data can be collected by airplanes, satellites, or sounding probes. One single satellite can cover the entire surface of the Earth. Precise information helps prevent meteorological catastrophes such as hurricanes or flooding.

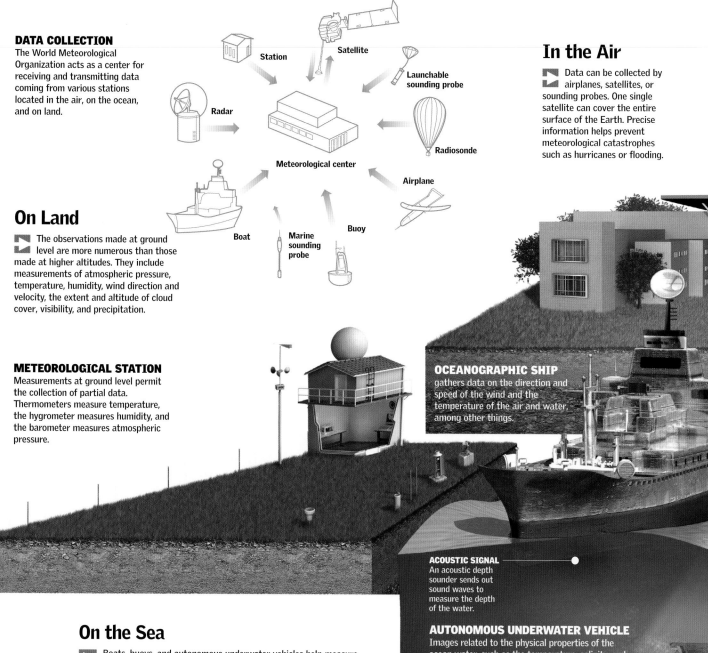

Station
Satellite
Launchable sounding probe
Radiosonde
Airplane
Buoy
Marine sounding probe
Boat
Meteorological center
Radar

OCEANOGRAPHIC SHIP

gathers data on the direction and speed of the wind and the temperature of the air and water, among other things.

ACOUSTIC SIGNAL
An acoustic depth sounder sends out sound waves to measure the depth of the water.

On the Sea

Boats, buoys, and autonomous underwater vehicles help measure water temperature, salinity, density, and reflected sunlight. All the information gathered is sent to a meteorological center.

AUTONOMOUS UNDERWATER VEHICLE
Images related to the physical properties of the ocean water, such as the temperature, salinity, and density, are relayed to operators and its location and depth tracked via the Global Positioning System (GPS).

RADIOSONDE

carries out airborne measurements of temperature, pressure, and relative humidity at different altitudes or atmospheric levels. It also indicates the direction and speed of the wind.

49,200 feet
(15,000 m)
is the altitude that a radiosonde can reach.

32,800 feet
(10,000 m)
The height at which they fly, near the upper limit of the troposphere

ARTIFICIAL SATELLITES

provide images used for visualizing clouds and water vapor in the atmosphere and for measuring the temperature of land and ocean surfaces.

49,200 feet
(13,000 m)
is the altitude that can be reached by the G-IV airplane.

METEOROLOGICAL AIRCRAFT

obtain temperature and humidity data and photograph particles contained in the clouds.

JET G-IV

Doppler radar

Parachutes
lengthen the time in the air.

Radiosonde
sends information to the base.

LAUNCHABLE SOUNDING PROBE

is launched from an airplane toward the ground. Its trajectory is followed as it relays information about wind velocity, temperature, humidity, and pressure.

HURRICANE HUNTER P-3 AIRPLANE

Its Doppler radar has a resolution four times greater than the standard Doppler radar in conventional use.

14,000 feet
(4,270 m)
is the altitude that can be reached by the P-3 aircraft.

AEROSON

1,200 feet
(365 m)
is the altitude that can be reached by a radio sounding probe.

AEROSONDE

Pilotless weather aircraft capable of sending meteorological information at intervals of tenths of a second

Better Forecasts

New models that measure changes in such variables as humidity, temperature, wind velocity, and cloud displacement may make it possible to improve forecasts by 25 percent over current ones.

CURRENT MODEL

Scale of 7 miles (12 km) per side

EXPERIMENTAL MODEL

Strongest winds. They are not detected by current models.

Scale of 1 mile (1.3 km) per side

METEOROLOGICAL CENTERS

They improve worldwide cooperation in meteorological observations, normalize the data obtained in different cities throughout the world, and promote the application of forecasts to various human activities.

Navigation lights
Anemometer
Data transmitter
Solar panel

METEOROLOGICAL BUOY

provides information about conditions of the sea in areas that are not covered by ships. The buoy floats freely with the ocean currents and transmits readings automatically via satellite.

6,600 feet
(2,000 m)
is the depth reached by the vehicle.

MARITIME SOUNDING PROBES

They are dropped from airplanes and then sink.

RADAR STATION

is utilized to measure the intensity with which rain, snow, or ice is falling. The radar sends radio waves that bounce off raindrops, and the return signal is displayed on a receiving screen.

Mobile Satellites

Meteorological satellites, which have been orbiting the Earth for more than 30 years, are an indispensable aid to scientists. Along with the images generated by these instruments, meteorologists receive data that can be used to prepare weather bulletins. These reports, circulated via the mass media, allow people all over the world to know the weather forecast. Moreover, the most advanced satellites are used to study the characteristics of phenomena such as tropical cyclones (hurricanes, cyclones, and typhoons). ●

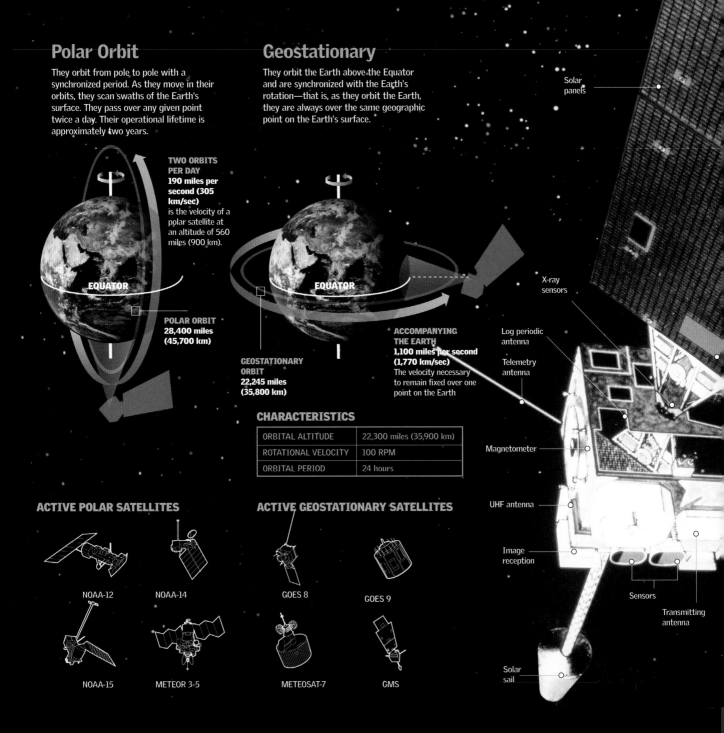

Polar Orbit

They orbit from pole to pole with a synchronized period. As they move in their orbits, they scan swaths of the Earth's surface. They pass over any given point twice a day. Their operational lifetime is approximately two years.

TWO ORBITS PER DAY
190 miles per second (305 km/sec) is the velocity of a polar satellite at an altitude of 560 miles (900 km).

EQUATOR

POLAR ORBIT
28,400 miles (45,700 km)

Geostationary

They orbit the Earth above the Equator and are synchronized with the Earth's rotation—that is, as they orbit the Earth, they are always over the same geographic point on the Earth's surface.

Solar panels

X-ray sensors

Log periodic antenna

Telemetry antenna

EQUATOR

ACCOMPANYING THE EARTH
1,100 miles per second (1,770 km/sec)
The velocity necessary to remain fixed over one point on the Earth

GEOSTATIONARY ORBIT
22,245 miles (35,800 km)

Magnetometer

UHF antenna

Image reception

Sensors

Transmitting antenna

Solar sail

CHARACTERISTICS

ORBITAL ALTITUDE	22,300 miles (35,900 km)
ROTATIONAL VELOCITY	100 RPM
ORBITAL PERIOD	24 hours

ACTIVE POLAR SATELLITES

NOAA-12

NOAA-14

NOAA-15

METEOR 3-5

ACTIVE GEOSTATIONARY SATELLITES

GOES 8

GOES 9

METEOSAT-7

GMS

Array
drive

GOES EAST

Orbital altitude	22,370 miles (36,000 km)
Weight	4,850 pounds (2,200 kg)
Launch date	2001
Orbit	75°

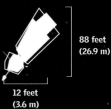

88 feet
(26.9 m)

12 feet
(3.6 m)

Images, Yesterday and Today

The TIROS satellites (Television and Infra-Red Observation Satellite) of the 1960s provided the first images of cloud systems. The modern GOES satellites (Geostationary Operational Environmental Satellites), which take more precise time and space measurements, provide higher-quality images of clouds, continents, and oceans. They also measure the humidity of the atmosphere and the temperature at ground level.

DARK ZONES
Low reflectivity

CLEAR ZONES
High
reflectivity

WHITE
High clouds

GREEN
Vegetation

YELLOW
Low clouds

VISIBLE IMAGE

Oceans and continents have low albedo and appear as darker areas. Areas with high albedo, in contrast, are clear and bright.

ORANGE
Dry and
mountainous

**AREA OF GREATEST
HEAT EMISSION**

COMBINED IMAGES

They are composed of infrared images (which permit differentiation of high and low clouds) and visible-light images (which measure the reflectivity of each climatic subsystem).

**AREA OF LEAST
HEAT EMISSION**

Receiving
antenna

INFRARED IMAGE

represents infrared emissions or heat from the clouds and from the Earth's surface. Objects that are hotter appear darker.

Climate Change

Mountain glaciers are melting, and this is a threat to the availability of freshwater. It is calculated that 8 cubic miles (35 cu km) of water melts from the glaciers each year, which is the glaciers' major contribution to raising the global sea level; it is thought that the continental ice sheet may play a significantly larger role. The volume of the glaciers in the

GLACIERS IN ALASKA
Approximately 5 percent of the land is
covered by glaciers, which advance and
break up when they reach the ocean,
where they form impressive cliffs of ice.

GODS AND RITUALS 76-77

CLIMATE ZONES 78-79

PALEOCLIMATOLOGY 80-81

THE PLANET WARMS UP 82-83

ACCELERATED MELTING 84-85

TOXIC RAIN 86-87

WEAKER AND WEAKER 88-89

CHANGE; EVERYTHING CHANGES 90-91

European Alps and in the Caucasus
Mountains has been reduced by half, and in
Africa, only 8 percent of the largest glacier of
Mount Kenya still exists. If these tendencies
continue, by the end of the century, most

glaciers will have disappeared completely,
including those in Glacier National Park in
the United States. That will have powerful
repercussions on the water resources of
many parts of the world. ●

Gods and Rituals

P redicting the weather was a subject of interest to all the early civilizations that populated the Earth. Greeks, Romans, Egyptians, pre-Columbians, and Orientals venerated the gods of the Sun, the Moon, the heavens, the rain, storms, and the wind for centuries. In their own way, with rituals and praise, they tried to influence the weather to improve the bounty of the harvest. ●

THE SCEPTER
A symbol of command consisting of ornamented short sticks, the symbol of authority

ZEPHYRUS
The Greek god of the west wind had an important presence. At times he was beneficial, and at other times catastrophic. Though the ancient Greeks were not sure whether the winds were male or female, they did believe the winds had wings.

The Romans

▶ The Romans worshiped many gods because they inherited them from the Greek oracles. The gods of weather were Jupiter (wise and just, who reigned over the earth), Apollo (the god of the sun), Neptune (the god of the sea and storms), and Saturn (the god of agriculture). Each god had a specific function. As a result, any human activity could suffer or benefit from the attitude of the god in charge of that particular function. Thus, the purpose of ritual worship and sacrifice to the gods was to gain their favor.

THE LIGHTNING BOLT
Jupiter reigned over the earth and heaven, and he had the attributes of an eagle, a lightning bolt, and a scepter.

Greeks

▶ The powerful Zeus was the king of the Greek gods and dispenser of divine justice. He was the sovereign of heaven (his brothers Poseidon and Hades governed the ocean and the underworld, respectively). He carried a thunderbolt to represent his power, associated with the weather. Zeus lived on Mount Olympus, from where he could observe and often intervene in the affairs of humans. The Greeks believed that Poseidon, when annoyed, would break up the mountains and throw them into the sea to form islands. Uranus was a personification of heaven for the Greeks, and Apollo was the god of the sun, light, and creation.

THE EAGLE
Jupiter is the Roman supreme god, represented by the figure of the eagle. He is also first in wisdom and power.

Egyptians

▶ As in all ancient civilizations, the gods of weather were very much a part of Egyptian life. Civilization extended along the banks of the Nile, where water was crucial for survival—that is, where cities, temples, pyramids, and the entire economic life of the kingdom were concentrated. The weather influenced the rising of the river and the harvests. Therefore the Egyptians venerated Re (the god of the sun), Nut (the god of heaven), Seth (the god of the storm), and Toth (the god of the moon).

RE
Egyptian sun god, the primordial creator. His center of worship was Heliopolis, or the City of the Sun.

SETH
Egyptian god of the storm, represented by a jackal, a dog, or a wolf. The son of Re and brother of Osiris.

Pre-Columbians

The pre-Columbian population believed water was a gift from the gods. For the Aztecs, Tlaloc was the god of rain, whereas the Incas called him Viracocha. Among the Mayans, he was known as Chac. He was the divinity of the peasants because water was the essential factor for stability and organization for these indigenous peoples. The calendar made it possible to forecast certain astrological events and rainstorms.

CHAC
Mayan god of agriculture. The Mayans performed ceremonies petitioning Chac for rain when drought threatened the harvest.

TLALOC
Venerated by the Aztecs, he was known as the provider because he had the power to bring rain, which made the corn grow.

VIRACOCHA
For the Incas, he was all powerful. Creator of the universe and of all the earth, he was linked with rays of light, thunder, lightning, and snow.

FUJIN
Japanese god of wind. Drawn as a dark monster, covered with leopard skin, he carried a bag of wind on his shoulders.

The Orient

Hinduism has various weather-related gods. The most popular is Surya (god of the sun). Next come Chandra (god of the moon), Indra (the god who governs heaven), and Parjanya (god of rain). Japanese mythology emphasizes the following: Fujin (god of wind), Amaterasu (goddess of the sun), Tsukiyomi (god of the moon), Amatsu-kami (god of heaven), Susanoo (god of storms), and Aji-Suki-Taka-Hi-Kone (god of thunder).

SURYA
Hindu god of the sun. In India the sun personified as Surya was considered to be harmful by the Dravidians of the south but benevolent by the peoples of central regions. These peoples attributed great healing power to the god.

Climate Zones

D ifferent places in the world, even if far removed from each other, can be grouped into climate zones—that is, into regions that are homogeneous relative to climatic elements, such as temperature, pressure, rain, and humidity. There is some disagreement among climatologists about the number and description of each of these regions, but the illustrations given on this map are generally accepted. ●

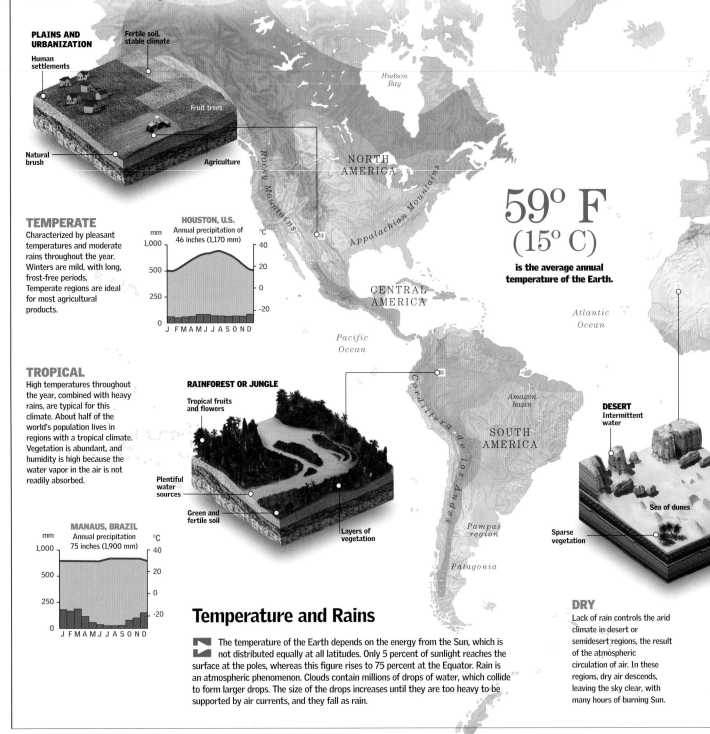

PLAINS AND URBANIZATION

Human settlements

Fertile soil, stable climate

Fruit trees

Natural brush

Agriculture

Ice cap

Hudson Bay

NORTH AMERICA

Rocky Mountains

Appalachian Mountains

TEMPERATE

Characterized by pleasant temperatures and moderate rains throughout the year. Winters are mild, with long, frost-free periods. Temperate regions are ideal for most agricultural products.

HOUSTON, U.S.
Annual precipitation of 46 inches (1,170 mm)

mm
1,000
500
250
0

°C
40
20
0
-20

J F M A M J J A S O N D

CENTRAL AMERICA

Pacific Ocean

Atlantic Ocean

59° F
(15° C)

is the average annual temperature of the Earth.

TROPICAL

High temperatures throughout the year, combined with heavy rains, are typical for this climate. About half of the world's population lives in regions with a tropical climate. Vegetation is abundant, and humidity is high because the water vapor in the air is not readily absorbed.

RAINFOREST OR JUNGLE

Tropical fruits and flowers

Plentiful water sources

Green and fertile soil

Layers of vegetation

Cordillera de los Andes

Amazon basin

SOUTH AMERICA

DESERT
Intermittent water

Sea of dunes

Sparse vegetation

MANAUS, BRAZIL
Annual precipitation 75 inches (1,900 mm)

mm
1,000
500
250
0

°C
40
20
0
-20

J F M A M J J A S O N D

Pampas region

Patagonia

Temperature and Rains

The temperature of the Earth depends on the energy from the Sun, which is not distributed equally at all latitudes. Only 5 percent of sunlight reaches the surface at the poles, whereas this figure rises to 75 percent at the Equator. Rain is an atmospheric phenomenon. Clouds contain millions of drops of water, which collide to form larger drops. The size of the drops increases until they are too heavy to be supported by air currents, and they fall as rain.

DRY

Lack of rain controls the arid climate in desert or semidesert regions, the result of the atmospheric circulation of air. In these regions, dry air descends, leaving the sky clear, with many hours of burning Sun.

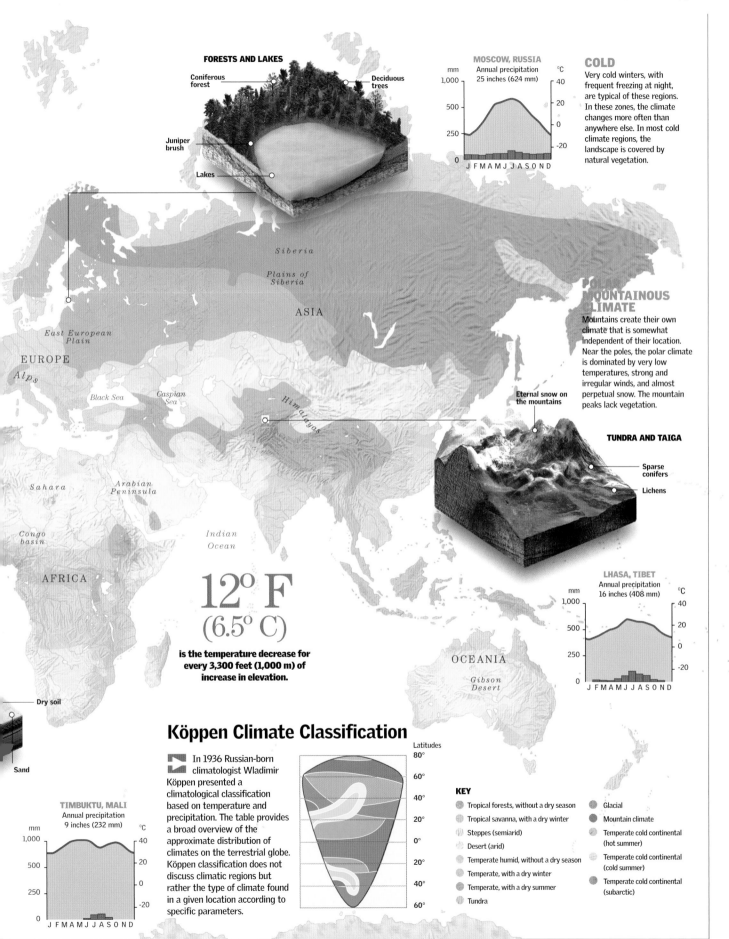

FORESTS AND LAKES

Coniferous forest

Deciduous trees

Juniper brush

Lakes

MOSCOW, RUSSIA
Annual precipitation
25 inches (624 mm)

mm
1,000
500
250
0
J F M A M J J A S O N D

°C
40
20
0
-20

COLD
Very cold winters, with frequent freezing at night, are typical of these regions. In these zones, the climate changes more often than anywhere else. In most cold climate regions, the landscape is covered by natural vegetation.

Siberia

Plains of Siberia

ASIA

POLAR MOUNTAINOUS CLIMATE
Mountains create their own climate that is somewhat independent of their location. Near the poles, the polar climate is dominated by very low temperatures, strong and irregular winds, and almost perpetual snow. The mountain peaks lack vegetation.

East European Plain

EUROPE

Alps

Black Sea

Caspian Sea

Himalayas

Eternal snow on the mountains

TUNDRA AND TAIGA

Sparse conifers

Lichens

Sahara

Arabian Peninsula

Congo basin

Indian Ocean

AFRICA

12° F
(6.5° C)
is the temperature decrease for every 3,300 feet (1,000 m) of increase in elevation.

LHASA, TIBET
Annual precipitation
16 inches (408 mm)

mm
1,000
500
250
0
J F M A M J J A S O N D

°C
40
20
0
-20

OCEANIA

Gibson Desert

Dry soil

Sand

Köppen Climate Classification

In 1936 Russian-born climatologist Wladimir Köppen presented a climatological classification based on temperature and precipitation. The table provides a broad overview of the approximate distribution of climates on the terrestrial globe. Köppen classification does not discuss climatic regions but rather the type of climate found in a given location according to specific parameters.

TIMBUKTU, MALI
Annual precipitation
9 inches (232 mm)

mm
1,000
500
250
0
J F M A M J J A S O N D

°C
40
20
0
-20

Latitudes
80°
60°
40°
20°
0°
20°
40°
60°

KEY

- Tropical forests, without a dry season
- Tropical savanna, with a dry winter
- Steppes (semiarid)
- Desert (arid)
- Temperate humid, without a dry season
- Temperate, with a dry winter
- Temperate, with a dry summer
- Tundra

- Glacial
- Mountain climate
- Temperate cold continental (hot summer)
- Temperate cold continental (cold summer)
- Temperate cold continental (subarctic)

Paleoclimatology

The climate of the planet is constantly changing. In approximately two million years, the Earth has gone through very cold periods, or glaciations, that lasted thousands of years, alternating with warm periods. Today we live in an interglacial period that began some 10,000 years ago with an increase in average global temperature. These climatic changes can be analyzed over time periods that exceed hundreds of thousands of years. Paleoclimatology uses records derived from fossils, tree rings, corals, glaciers, and historical documents to study the climates of the past. ●

VOSTOK

Latitude 77° S
Longitude 105° E

Surface area of the lake	5,405 square miles (14,000 sq km)
Inhabitants	Only scientists
Year of founding	1957
Temperature	-67° F (-55° C)
Surface	95% ice

Gas Measurement

Vertical ice cores (or samples) allow scientists to study the climate of the past. The nearly 12-foot-long (3.6-m) ice sample taken at the Russian Vostok station contains climatic data going back 420,000 years, including the concentration of carbon dioxide, methane, and other greenhouse gases in the atmosphere.

SAMPLES
The zones marked on the map are places where scientists have gathered samples of ice, which were analyzed in the laboratories.

Dronning Maud Land

VOSTOK

Siple Station   ● South Pole

RIDS   ● Dominion Range

● Law Dome

Little America   ● Newall glacier
● Talos Dome

KEY
● Drillings
▢ Ice sheets

Chronology

During the history of the Earth, climate has changed greatly, which has had a large effect not only on the appearance of the Earth's surface but also on animal and plant life. This timeline shows the planet's major climate changes and their consequences.

B.Y.A. = billions of years ago   M.Y.A. = millions of years ago   Y.A. = years ago

4.5 B.Y.A.
In the beginning, there was heat. Life produces oxygen and cools the climate.

2.7-1.8 B.Y.A.
Ice covers very extensive areas.

544 M.Y.A.
Glacial climate in a changing geography. Extinction of 70 percent of marine species.

330 M.Y.A.
Beginning of a long period of glaciation. Ice covers different geographic areas.

245 M.Y.A.
Drought and heat at the beginning. Abrupt cooling at the end of the period. Appearance of the dinosaurs.

65 M.Y.A.
Paleocene and beginning Eocene: very warm climate. Middle Eocene: cooling begins.

Human Activity

Climate can be divided into before and after the Industrial Revolution. This graphic shows the progressive increase of halocarbon gases, methane, carbon dioxide, and nitrous oxide between 1770 and 1990. It is clear that humans have contributed to the contamination of the planet.

EVALUATION OF GREENHOUSE GASES

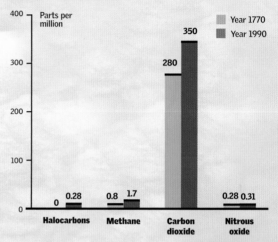

CLOTHES
protect the scientists from the weather and prevent the contamination of samples.

Composition

The lower graphic shows the change in concentration of methane in the atmosphere in the last 20,000 years until the end of the preindustrial era. The information collected was estimated on the basis of ice probes in Greenland and Antarctica.

METHANE CONCENTRATION

ICE CORES
Samples are taken at different depths. The surface snow becomes more compact in the lower layers. In the last layer, there are rocks and sand.

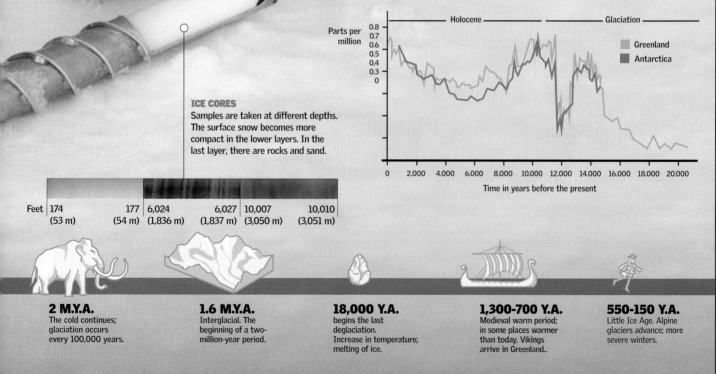

| Feet | 174 (53 m) | 177 (54 m) | 6,024 (1,836 m) | 6,027 (1,837 m) | 10,007 (3,050 m) | 10,010 (3,051 m) |

2 M.Y.A.
The cold continues; glaciation occurs every 100,000 years.

1.6 M.Y.A.
Interglacial. The beginning of a two-million-year period.

18,000 Y.A.
begins the last deglaciation. Increase in temperature; melting of ice.

1,300-700 Y.A.
Medieval warm period; in some places warmer than today. Vikings arrive in Greenland..

550-150 Y.A.
Little Ice Age. Alpine glaciers advance; more severe winters.

The Planet Warms Up

The increase in average temperature of the Earth's atmosphere and oceans is the result of global warming. The main cause is an increase in carbon dioxide emissions by industrialized nations during the past 200 years. This phenomenon has increased the greenhouse effect. It is estimated that the average global temperature has increased more than 1.1° F (0.6° C) between the end of the 19th century and the year 2000. The consequences of this are already beginning to be noticed. Changes are observed in the global distribution of precipitation: there are regions where there is an increase of rain, and there are other regions where rain is diminishing. This generates, among other things, a redistribution of fauna and flora, changes in ecosystems, and changes in human activities.

Product of Human Activity

Our planet is going through an accelerated process of global warming because of the accumulation in the atmosphere of a series of gases generated by human activity. These gases not only absorb the energy emitted by the surface of the Earth when it is heated by radiation coming from the Sun, but they also strengthen the naturally occurring greenhouse effect, whose purpose is to trap heat. One of the primary agents responsible for the growth of the greenhouse effect is CO_2 (carbon dioxide), which is artificially produced by burning fossil fuels (coal, petroleum, and natural gas). Because of the intensive use of these fuels, there has been a notable increase in the quantity of both carbon and nitrogen oxides and carbon dioxide released into the atmosphere. Other aggravating human activities, such as deforestation, have limited the regenerative capacity of the atmosphere to eliminate carbon dioxide through photosynthesis. These changes have caused a slow increase in the average annual temperature of the Earth. Global warming, in turn, causes numerous environmental problems: desertification and droughts (which cause famines), deforestation (which further increases climate change), floods, and the destruction of ecosystems. Because all these variables contribute to global warming in complex ways, it is very difficult to predict with precision everything that will happen in the future.

84° F
(29° C)

The discoloration of coral occurs when the temperature exceeds 84° F (29° C). Algae are lost, the coral weakens, and the color of the coral fades.

1

Activities, such as the burning of fuels and deforestation, increase the concentration of greenhouse gases.

INCREASE OF PRIMARY GREENHOUSE GASES

Stratopause
STRATOSPHERE
Tropopause
LOW TROPOSPHERE

THE TEMPERATURE OF THE EARTH THROUGH THE YEARS

The effects of global warming are already noticeable. It is estimated that the average global temperature has increased more than 1.1° F (0.6° C) between the end of the 19th century and the year 2000.

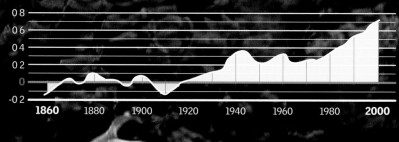

0 8		
0 6		
0 4		
0 2		
0		
-0 2		
1860 1880 1900 1920 1940 1960 1980 2000		

GREAT BARRIER REEF

Latitude 18°S

Longitude 147°E

Surface	1,430 miles (2,300 km)
Types of reefs	3,000
Age	300 million years
Discovery	1770, by James Cook

1.1° F
(0.6° C)
APPROXIMATE INCREASE
Of the Earth's global average temperature from 1860

A Different World

With the changing patterns of precipitation and the shifting of air-pressure systems, some regions will become more humid, and others will suffer droughts. One of the areas that will become drier will be the western part of North America, where desertification is already affecting agriculture. According to current forecasts, areas in high latitudes, closer to the poles, will go through a rapid warming in the next 40 years. Populations of animals will be forced to emigrate from their habitat to avoid extinction, and other animals, such as the polar bear and emperor penguin, will have trouble subsisting as their habitats disappear. Ocean levels are rising between 0.4 and 0.8 inch (1 and 2 cm) per decade. Some Pacific island nations such as Tuvalu have contingency plans for evacuation. Another affected region is the Great Barrier Reef of Australia. The coral is very sensitive to changes in temperature. At temperatures above a normal 84° F [29 ° C], the coral begin to expel the algae on which they depend for food, and then they die.

2 Increase of the natural greenhouse effect of the atmosphere

3 The modified atmosphere retains more heat emitted by the Earth and thus upsets the natural equilibrium.

SOLAR ENERGY

ATMOSPHERE

OZONE

The ozone layer is in the stratosphere, above the surface of the planet. It acts as a powerful solar filter that prevents the passage of all but a small amount of ultraviolet radiation (UV).

Ozone layer

2 km   10 km

Accelerated Melting

The climate is changing at a disconcerting speed. Glaciers are retreating, and sea level is rising because of a phenomenon known as thermal expansion. Scientists evaluating the planet's health deduce that this is the consequence of the Earth warming too rapidly. Human activity—in particular, the burning of fossil fuels and the consequent accumulation of greenhouse gases in the atmosphere—has increased this trend. ●

ARCTIC
Latitude 66° N
Longitude 0°

Surface area	5,444,040 square miles (14,100,000 sq km)
Depth	13,100 to 6,600 feet (4,000 to 2,000 m)
Temperature	-58° F (-50° C) in winter

Why It Happens

➤ The thawing at the poles is, in part, caused by the increase of greenhouse gases. They absorb the radiation emitted by the Earth and heat up the atmosphere, further increasing the Earth's temperature. The melting of glaciers puts more water in the oceans.

EFFECT
The Arctic heats up more rapidly than the global average because of the darkness of the soil and the water, which, once exposed, trap more heat from the atmosphere.

5. Once exposed to the air, the CO_2 is absorbed by the atmosphere.

1. Sunlight reflects from layers of ice.

2. Where the ice is the thinnest, or cracked, radiation penetrates to the ocean.

3. Ice absorbs the heat from sunlight and releases a great quantity of trapped carbon particles.

4. These particles rise to the surface, converted into CO_2.

Via cracks in the ice, new marine routes can develop. When ships pass, the cracks rarely close, increasing the process of heat absorption and the release of CO_2.

Particles of CO_2

Pacific Ocean

Bering Strait

OCEAN CURRENTS
The main cause of changes in ocean currents are changes in the water's salinity.

North America

Hudson Bay

Greenland

Atlantic Ocean

80%
of Greenland's ice is losing 3 feet (1 m) per year.

PROJECTIONS 2010-30

Summer sea ice, currently in decline, tends to diminish more and more rapidly in the future.

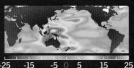
2040-60

As the century progresses, sea ice continues to melt more and more along the coasts of the Arctic Ocean.

2070-90

Some scientific models project that summer sea ice will be virtually eliminated during this century.

Europe

ADVANCE OF VEGETATION

The retreat of the ice leaves organic material exposed, which, instead of reflecting solar radiation, absorbs it, increasing global temperature.

LABRADOR CURRENT

starts in the Arctic and moves south, carrying cold water and loose ice.

Barents Sea

Melting of the ice will be detrimental to people and animals living in the Arctic.

TEMPERATURE INCREASE

It is believed that the increased emission of greenhouse gases will cause an increase in average global temperature of between 3.2° and 7.2° F (1.8° and 4.0° C) over the next 100 years.

ADVANCING WATERS

The accelerated melting raises sea level and floods coasts that have a gentle slope. As the sea level rises, the width of coastal areas diminishes.

50 m

50 cm

164 feet (50 m)

The amount of coastal area lost when sea level rises 20 inches (50 cm)

70%

of the freshwater in the world is in Antarctica.

GULF STREAM

originates in the Gulf of Mexico and carries warm water to higher latitudes.

Antarctica

The Antarctic loses 36 cubic miles (152 cu km) of ice per year, and the western ice sheet is becoming thinner at an accelerating pace. This is contributing to increases in sea level. Over the long term, the effect on the climate could be disastrous for many regions of the planet.

Toxic Rain

Burning fossil fuel releases into the air chemicals that mix with water vapor and produce acid rain. The excess of sulfur dioxides and nitrogen dioxides in bodies of water makes the development of aquatic life more difficult, substantially increasing the mortality rate of fish. Likewise, it affects vegetation on land, causing significant damage in forested areas by contaminating animals and destroying substances vital for the soil. Moreover, acidic sedimentation can increase the levels of toxic metals, such as aluminum, copper, and mercury, that are deposited in untreated drinking-water reservoirs. ●

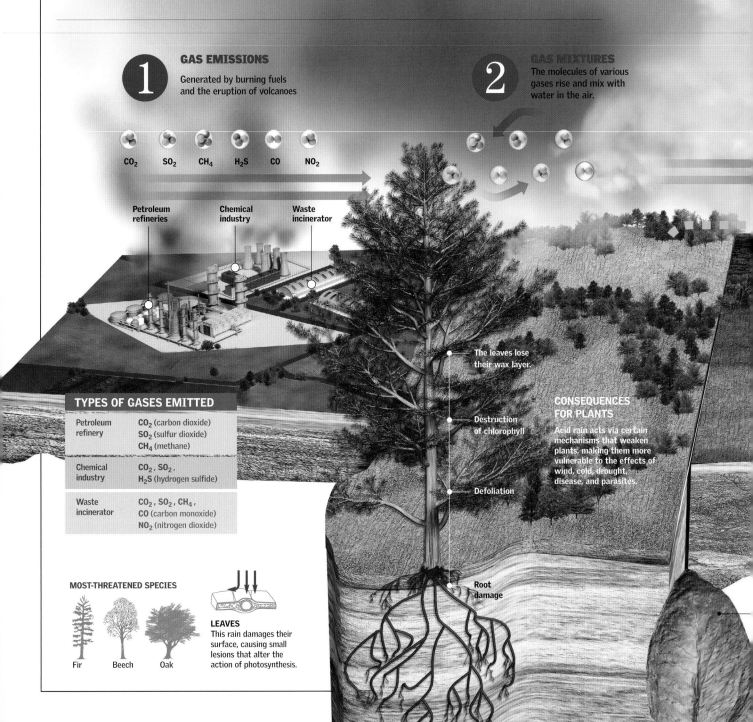

1 GAS EMISSIONS
Generated by burning fuels and the eruption of volcanoes

2 GAS MIXTURES
The molecules of various gases rise and mix with water in the air.

CO_2 SO_2 CH_4 H_2S CO NO_2

Petroleum refineries

Chemical industry

Waste incinerator

The leaves lose their wax layer.

Destruction of chlorophyll

CONSEQUENCES FOR PLANTS
Acid rain acts via certain mechanisms that weaken plants, making them more vulnerable to the effects of wind, cold, drought, disease, and parasites.

Defoliation

Root damage

TYPES OF GASES EMITTED

Petroleum refinery	CO_2 (carbon dioxide) SO_2 (sulfur dioxide) CH_4 (methane)
Chemical industry	CO_2, SO_2, H_2S (hydrogen sulfide)
Waste incinerator	CO_2, SO_2, CH_4, CO (carbon monoxide) NO_2 (nitrogen dioxide)

MOST-THREATENED SPECIES

Fir   Beech   Oak

LEAVES
This rain damages their surface, causing small lesions that alter the action of photosynthesis.

AREAS AFFECTED BY ACID RAIN

The regions most vulnerable to this phenomenon are Mexico, Beijing, Cairo, Jakarta (Indonesia), and Los Angeles.

③ PHOTOCHEMICAL REACTION

Sunlight increases the speed at which chemical reactions occur. Thus, sulfur dioxide and atmospheric gases rapidly produce sulfur trioxide.

Atmospheric circulation enhances the dispersal of contaminants over great distances.

④ ACID RAIN

falls in the form of water, fog, or dew and leaves the acids formed in the atmosphere on the ground.

pH:5
Acid rain

pH:6
Normal rain

pH acid

| pH 4.0 |
| pH 5.0 |
| pH 5.5 |
| pH 6.0 |
| pH 6.5 |

pH neutral

| pH 7.0 |

WHAT IS pH?

The degree of acidity of an aqueous solution. It indicates the concentration of hydrogen ions.

SOIL CONSEQUENCES

SILICATE SOIL
The effect of acidity increases because of the lack of buffering minerals.

CALCAREOUS SOIL
The effect is neutralized by the presence of bicarbonate.

CONSEQUENCES FOR AGRICULTURE

Areas under cultivation are not as vulnerable because they are generally improved by fertilizers that restore nutrients to the soil and neutralize acidity.

Melting water carries acidic particles that come from the rain.

EFFECTS ON THE WATER

The acidity of rainwater changes the neutral pH of bodies of water.

pH 7 → pH 4.3
(neutral)   (acid)

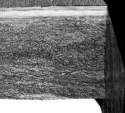
Seriously affected species are lettuce and tobacco, especially because their leaves, destined for human consumption, must be of high quality.

In mountainous areas, fog and snow contribute significant quantities of the gases in question.

1972 The year when the phenomenon of acid rain was recorded for the first time

pH 4.3 LEVEL AT WHICH FISH DO NOT SURVIVE IN THE WATER

MOST-AFFECTED SPECIES

Trout   Perch   Frogs

Weaker and Weaker

Artificial substances are destroying the ozone layer, which provides protection against ultraviolet rays. This phenomenon is observed every year in polar regions (primarily in the Antarctic) between August and October. Because of this, the Earth is receiving more harmful rays, which perhaps explains the appearance of certain illnesses: an increase in skin cancer cases, damage to vision, and weakening of the immune system. ●

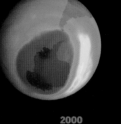

2000
11,000,000 square miles
(28,000,000 sq km)

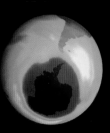

2001
10,000,000 square miles
(26,000,000 sq km)

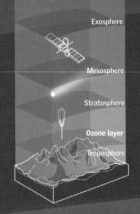

Exosphere

Mesosphere

Stratosphere

Ozone layer

Troposphere

OZONE LAYER

At an altitude of 12 to 19 miles (20 to 30 km), the Earth is surrounded by a stratospheric ozone layer that is of vital importance for life on the surface. The layer is formed from oxygen molecules through the absorption of ultraviolet light from the Sun. This reaction is reversible, that is, the ozone can return to its natural state, oxygen. This oxygen is reconverted into ozone, beginning a continuous process of formation and destruction of these components.

It is popularly called the ozone hole—a decrease or abnormal thinning that occurs in the ozone layer.

HOW IT DETERIORATES

1 Ultraviolet radiation strikes a molecule of CFC gas.

2 An atom of chlorine is released.

HOW OZONE IS FORMED

1 Ultraviolet rays strike a molecule of oxygen which breaks up and releases its two atoms.

2 One of the released atoms combines with a molecule of oxygen. Together they form a molecule of ozone.

3 One of the released atoms combines with a molecule of oxygen. Together they form a molecule of ozone.

4 The process can start again with the new oxygen molecule.

O_2

O_3

CFC GASES

are a family of gases with multiple applications. They are used in refrigeration systems, air-conditioning equipment, and aerosols.

WHEN? WHO? HOW?

In 1974, it was discovered that industrial chlorofluorocarbons (CFCs) affect the ozone layer. Chemists Mario Molina and F. Sherwood Rowland demonstrated that industrial CFCs are the gases that weaken the ozone layer by destroying the ozone molecules.

UV RADIATION

Ultraviolet radiation (UV) is a radiant form of energy that comes from the Sun. The various forms of radiation are classified according to the average wavelength measured in nanometers (nm), equivalent to one millionth of a millimeter. The shorter the wavelength, the greater the energy of the radiation.

UV-A
These rays easily penetrate the ozone layer. They cause skin wrinkling and aging.

UV-B
are almost all absorbed by the ozone layer. They are harmful and cause various types of skin cancer.

UV-C
These are the most damaging rays, but they are totally filtered by the upper part of the ozone layer.

2004
9,300,000 square miles
(24,200,000 sq km)

2005
10,400,000 square miles
(27,000,000 sq km)

THE SOUTHERN OZONE HOLE
The thinning of the ozone layer over the Antarctic is the result of a series of phenomena, including the action of chlorine radicals, which cause the destruction of ozone.

11,000,000
square miles
(28,000,000 sq km)
is the size of the area of attenuated ozone reached in 2000.

The ozone layer functions as a natural filter, absorbing UV rays.

75%
OF SKIN CANCER IS ATTRIBUTED TO UV-B RADIATION.

3 Chlorine atoms combine with a molecule of ozone, destroy it, and form one chloromonoxide and one oxygen atom.

4 The chloromonoxide combines with an atom of free oxygen and releases the chlorine atom.

5 This atom, once again free, combines with another molecule of ozone.

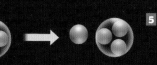

50 to 100
THE NUMBER OF YEARS THAT CFC GASES SURVIVE IN THE ATMOSPHERE

HUMAN BEINGS
Skin cancer. Damage to vision. Weakening of the immune system. Severe burns. Skin aging.

PLANTS
Destruction of phytoplankton. Inhibition of the photosynthesis process. Changes in growth. Reduced harvest yields.

ANIMALS
Diseases among farm animals. Destruction of links in the food chain. Increase of skin cancer.

Change; Everything Changes

Atlantic Ocean

NORTH AMERICA

The Most Responsible

▶ The climate of the planet is constantly changing. At present, the average global temperature is approximately 59° F (15° C). Geologic and other types of evidence suggest that in the past the average could have been as low as 45° F (7° C) and as high as 81° F (27° C). Climate change is, in large part, caused by human activities, which cause an increase in the concentration of greenhouse gases. These gases include carbon dioxide, methane, and nitrogen dioxide and are released by modern industry, by agriculture, and by the burning of coal, petroleum, and natural gas. Its atmospheric concentration is increasing: atmospheric carbon-dioxide content alone has grown by more than 20 percent since 1960. Investigators indicate that this warming can have grave implications for the stability of the climate, on which most of the life on the planet depends.

THE RISE IN TEMPERATURE
In Alaska and western Canada winter temperatures have increased between 5.4° and 7.2° F (3° and 4° C) in the past 50 years. It has been projected that in the next 100 years the Earth's average temperature will increase between 3.2° and 7.2° F (1.8° and 4.0° C).

CENTRAL AMERICA

Pacific Ocean

From 3.6° to 5.4° F (2° to 3° C)

SOUTH AMERICA

From 1.8° to 3.6° F (1° to 2° C)

Normal thickness of the ozone layer

Hole in the ozone

The ozone layer stops ultraviolet rays.

Rays that pass through the ozone layer

SURFACE OF THE EARTH

THE ICY COASTLINE

THINNING OF THE OZONE LAYER
The ozone layer protects us from ultraviolet rays, but, because of the release of artificial substances, it is thinning out. This phenomenon is observed each year over Antarctica between August and October and over the North Pole between October and May. Moreover, there is evidence that greater amounts of UV rays at the Earth's surface are destroying or altering vegetable cells and decreasing the production of oxygen.

THE EFFECT OF POLAR MELTING
The snow-covered sea ice reflects between 85 and 90 percent of the sunlight that strikes it, whereas sea water reflects only 10 percent. For that reason, as the ice and snow melt, many of today's coastlines will become submerged under water, which will cause yet more ice to melt.

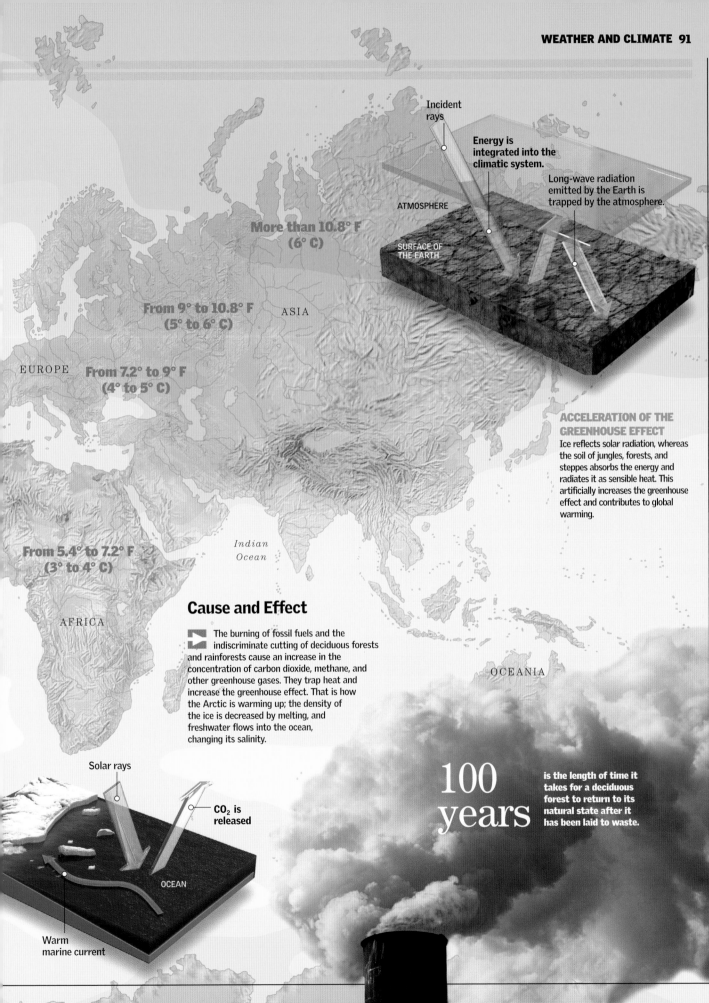

Incident rays

Energy is integrated into the climatic system.

Long-wave radiation emitted by the Earth is trapped by the atmosphere.

ATMOSPHERE

SURFACE OF THE EARTH

More than 10.8° F (6° C)

From 9° to 10.8° F (5° to 6° C)

ASIA

EUROPE   From 7.2° to 9° F (4° to 5° C)

ACCELERATION OF THE GREENHOUSE EFFECT
Ice reflects solar radiation, whereas the soil of jungles, forests, and steppes absorbs the energy and radiates it as sensible heat. This artificially increases the greenhouse effect and contributes to global warming.

From 5.4° to 7.2° F (3° to 4° C)

Indian Ocean

AFRICA

Cause and Effect

The burning of fossil fuels and the indiscriminate cutting of deciduous forests and rainforests cause an increase in the concentration of carbon dioxide, methane, and other greenhouse gases. They trap heat and increase the greenhouse effect. That is how the Arctic is warming up; the density of the ice is decreased by melting, and freshwater flows into the ocean, changing its salinity.

OCEANIA

Solar rays

CO_2 is released

100 years

is the length of time it takes for a deciduous forest to return to its natural state after it has been laid to waste.

OCEAN

Warm marine current

Glossary

Accretion

Growth of an ice crystal in the atmosphere by direct capture of water droplets when the temperature is below 32° F (0° C).

Acid Rain

Rain resulting from the mixture of water vapor in the air with chemical substances typically released by the combustion of fossil fuels.

Aerosol

Aerosols are very small (liquid or solid) particles suspended in the atmosphere, with varied chemical composition. Aerosols play an essential role in the formation of clouds by acting as condensation nuclei. They are also important to the Earth's radiation balance since they help to increase the reflection and dispersion of radiation coming from the Sun.

Air Mass

Extensive volume in the atmosphere whose physical properties, in particular the temperature and humidity in a horizontal plane, show only small and gradual differences. An air mass can cover an area of a few million square miles and can have a thickness of several miles.

Albedo

A measure of the percentage of radiation reflected by a surface.

Altitude

Height relative to sea level.

Anemometer

Instrument for measuring wind velocity.

Anticyclone

Region where the atmospheric pressure is relatively high compared with neighboring regions. Normally the air above an anticyclone descends, which prevents clouds from forming at medium and high levels of the atmosphere. Hence an anticyclonic system is associated with good weather.

Atmosphere

The gaseous envelope that surrounds the Earth.

Atmospheric Pressure

The pressure or weight exerted by the atmosphere at a specific point. Its measurement can be expressed in various units: hectopascals, millibars, inches, or millimeters of mercury (Hg). It is also called barometric pressure.

Aurora

A phenomenon that is produced in the higher layers of the atmosphere at polar latitudes. An aurora occurs when there is a collision between the electrically charged particles emitted by the Sun and the magnetic field of the Earth. In the Northern Hemisphere, the phenomenon is called the aurora borealis, and in the Southern Hemisphere, it is known as the aurora australis.

Avalanche

A large mass of snow that flows down the side of a mountain.

Barometer

An instrument for measuring atmospheric pressure. A decrease in pressure usually means that storms are on the way. Increasing pressure indicates good weather.

Beaufort Scale

A scale invented at the beginning of the 19th century by a British sailor, Francis Beaufort, for estimating and reporting wind velocity. It is based on the different shapes taken by water waves at different wind velocities, and its graduation goes from 0 to 12. There is also a Beaufort scale for application on land based on observations of the wind's effect on trees and other objects.

Carbon Dioxide

An odorless, colorless gas emitted in the engine exhaust of automobiles, trucks, and buses. It is also produced by the combustion of coal and other organic material. Too much carbon dioxide in the atmosphere contributes to global warming.

Chlorofluorocarbons

Artificial chemical substances often contained in aerosols, refrigerants, and air conditioners. These chemicals are largely responsible for the damage to the ozone layer.

Cirrus

Wispy cloud formations at altitudes greater than 16,400 feet (5,000 m).

Climate

The average state of the meteorological conditions of a location considered over a long period of time. The climate of a location is determined by climatological factors: latitude, longitude, altitude, topography, and continentality.

Cloud

A visible mass of small particles, such as droplets of water and/or crystals of ice, suspended in the air. A cloud is formed in the atmosphere because of the condensation of water vapor onto solid particles of smoke, dust, ashes, and other elements called condensation nuclei.

Coalescence

The process of growth of drops of water in a cloud. Two drops collide and remain joined after the collision, constituting a bigger drop. This is one of the mechanisms that explains the growth of the size of drops in a cloud until precipitation (rain) is produced.

Cold Wave

A rapid drop in temperature to the point requiring special protective measures in agriculture, industry, commerce, or social activities.

Condensation

The process by which water vapor is transformed into liquid by the effect of cooling.

Conduction

The transfer of heat through a substance by molecular action or from one substance to another it is in contact with.

Continentality

The tendency of the interior regions of the continents to have more extreme temperature changes than coastal zones.

Convection

The process by which a heated surface transfers energy to the material (air, water, etc.) above it. This material becomes less dense and rises. Cooler material descends to fill in the void. Air rising as a result of the heating of the ground by the Sun's rays.

Coriolis Force

A fictitious or apparent force that applies when the Earth is used as a reference frame for motion. It depends upon the latitude and the velocity of the object in motion. In the Northern Hemisphere, the air is deflected toward the right side of its path, and in the Southern Hemisphere, the air is deflected toward the left side of its path. This force is strongest at the poles and does not exist at the Equator.

Cyclone

A climatic low-pressure system.

Desert

A hot or cold zone where annual precipitation is less than 1 inch (25 mm).

Desertification

A process that converts fertile land to desert through a reduction in precipitation.

Dew

Condensation in the form of small drops of water formed on grass and other small objects near the ground when the temperature has dropped to the dew point. This generally happens during the night.

Dike

An earthwork for containing or channeling a river or for protection against the sea.

Drizzle

A type of light liquid precipitation composed of small drops with diameters between 0.007 and 0.019 inch (0.2 and 0.5 mm). Usually drizzle falls from stratus-type clouds that are found at low altitudes and can be accompanied by fog, which significantly decreases visibility.

Drought

An abnormally dry climatic condition in a specific area where the lack of water is prolonged and which causes a serious hydrological imbalance.

El Niño

The anomalous appearance, every few years, of unusually warm ocean conditions along the tropical west coast of South America.

Erosion

Action in which the ground is worn down by moving water, glaciers, wind, or waves.

Evaporation

Physical process by which a liquid (such as water) is transformed into its gaseous state (such as water vapor). The reverse process is called condensation.

Exosphere

The outermost layer of the Earth's atmosphere.

Flash Flood

Sudden flooding caused by the passage of a large quantity of water through a narrow space, such as a canyon or a valley.

Fog

Visible manifestation of drops of water suspended in the atmosphere at or near ground level; this reduces the horizontal visibility to less than a mile. It originates when the temperature of the air is near the dew point, and sufficient numbers of condensation nuclei are present.

Forecast

A statement about future events. The weather forecast includes the use of objective models based on a number of atmospheric parameters combined with the ability and experience of the meteorologist. It is also called weather prediction.

Front

The transition or contact zone between two masses of air with different meteorological characteristics, which almost always implies different temperatures. For example, a front occurs at the area of convergence between warm humid air and dry cold air.

Frontogenesis

The process of formation or intensification of a front. This happens when wind forces two adjacent masses of air of different densities and temperatures together, creating a front. It can occur when one of the masses of air, or both, move over a surface that reinforces their original properties. This is common on the east coast of North America or Asia, when a mass of air moving toward the ocean has a weak or undefined boundary. It is the opposite of frontolysis.

Frost

A covering of ice crystals on a cold object.

Global Warming

The heating of the atmosphere caused by increased concentrations of greenhouse gases due to human activities.

Greenhouse Effect

A phenomenon explained by the presence of certain components in the atmosphere (primarily carbon dioxide [CO_2], water vapor, and ozone) that absorb a portion of the infrared radiation emitted by the surface of the Earth and simultaneously reflect radiative energy back to the surface. This process contributes to the increase in the average temperature near the surface.

Gust

A rapid and significant increase in wind velocity. The maximum velocity of the wind must reach at least 16 knots (18 miles per hour [30 km/h]), and the difference between the peaks and calm must be at least 10 knots (12 miles per hour [18 km/h]). It generally lasts less than 20 seconds.

Hail

Precipitation that originates in convective clouds, such as the cumulonimbus, in the form of masses or irregular pieces of ice. Typically hail has a diameter of 0.2 to 2 inches (5 to 50 mm) but may grow significantly larger. The smallest ice fragments—whose diameter is 0.2 inch (5 mm) or less—are called small hailstones, or graupel. Strong upward currents are required inside the clouds for hail to be produced.

Heat Wave

A period of abnormally hot and uncomfortable weather. It can last from a few days to a number of weeks.

Hectopascal

A pressure unit equal to 100 pascals and equivalent to 1 millibar—a millibar being equivalent to 0.031 inch (0.8 mm) of ordinary mercury. The millibar (mb) was the technical unit used to measure pressure until recently, when the hectopascal was adopted. The pascal is the unit for pressure in the MKS system, corresponding to the pressure exerted by the unit force (1 newton) on a unit surface (1 square meter—11 square feet); 1,000 hPa = 1,000 mb = 1 bar = 14.5 pounds per square inch.

High

A prefix describing cloud formations at an altitude between 6,560 and 16,400 feet (2,000 and 5,000 m).

Humidity

The amount of water vapor contained in the air.

Hurricane

The name for a tropical cyclone with sustained winds of 64 knots (74 miles per hour [119 km/h]) or more, which develops in the North Atlantic, the Caribbean, the Gulf of Mexico, and the Pacific Northeast. This storm is called a typhoon in the western Pacific and a cyclone in the Indian Ocean.

Hygrometer

An instrument used to measure humidity.

Ice

The solid state of water. It is found in the atmosphere in the form of ice crystals, snow, or hail.

Jet Streams

Air currents high in the troposphere (about 6 miles [10 km] above sea level), where the wind velocity can be up to 90 meters per second (200 miles per hour). This type of structure is seen in subtropical latitudes in both hemispheres, where the flow is toward the east, reaching its maximum intensity during the winter.

Latitude

A system of imaginary parallel lines that encircle the globe north and south of the Equator. The poles are located at 90° latitude north and south and the Equator at 0° latitude.

Lightning

A discharge of the atmosphere's static electricity occurring between a cloud and the ground.

Mesosphere

The layer of the Earth's atmosphere that lies above the stratosphere.

METAR

The name of the format airport meteorological bulletins are reported in. This includes data on wind, visibility, temperature, dew point, and atmospheric pressure, among other variables.

Meteorology

The science and study of atmospheric phenomena. Some of the subdivisions of meteorology are agrometeorology, climatology, hydrometeorology, and physical, dynamic, and synoptic meteorology.

Microbarometer

A very sensitive barometer that records pressure variations using a magnified scale.

Mist

Microscopic drops of water suspended in the air, or humid hygroscopic particles, which reduce visibility at ground level.

Monsoon

A seasonal wind that causes heavy rains in tropical and subtropical regions.

Normal

The standard value accepted for a meteorological element as calculated for a specific location over a specific number of years. The normal values refer to the distribution of data within the limits of the common occurrence. The parameters can include temperature (high, low, and divergences), pressure, precipitation (rain, snow, etc.), winds (velocity and direction), storms, cloud cover, percentage of relative humidity, and so on.

Ocean Current

The movement of water in the ocean caused by the system of planetary winds. Ocean currents transport warm or cold water over long distances around the planet.

Orographic Rain

Rain that results from the cooling of humid air as it crosses over a mountain range.

Ozone Layer

A layer of the atmosphere situated 20 to 30 miles (30 to 50 km) above the Earth's surface between the troposphere and the stratosphere. It acts as a filtering mechanism for ultraviolet radiation.

Polar Front

An almost permanent and very large front of the middle latitudes that separates the relatively cold polar air and the relatively warm subtropical air.

Precipitation

A liquid or solid, crystallized or amorphous particle that falls from a cloud or system of clouds and reaches the ground.

Radiation

The process by which energy propagates through a specific medium (or a vacuum) via wave phenomena or motion. Electromagnetic radiation, which emits heat and light, is one form of radiation. Other forms are sound waves.

Seaquake

An earthquake at the bottom of the ocean, causing a violent agitation of ocean waves, which in some cases reach coastal areas and cause flooding.

Snow

Precipitation in the form of white or transparent frozen ice crystals, often in the form of complex hexagons. In general, snow falls from stratiform clouds, but it can also fall from cumulus clouds, usually in the form of snowflakes.

Stratosphere

The layer of the atmosphere situated above the troposphere.

Stratus

Low clouds that form layers. They often produce drizzle.

Synoptic Map

A map that shows weather conditions of the Earth's surface at a certain time and place.

Thermal Inversion

An inversion of the normal reduction in temperature with an increase in altitude.

Thermometer

An instrument for measuring temperature. The different scales used in meteorology are Celsius, Fahrenheit, and Kelvin (or absolute).

Tornado

A column of air that rotates with great violence, stretching between a convective cloud and the surface of the Earth. It is the most destructive phenomenon in the atmosphere. Tornadoes can occur, under the right conditions, anywhere on Earth, but they appear most frequently in the central United States, between the Rocky Mountains and the Appalachian Mountains.

Tropical Cyclone

A cyclone without fronts, it develops over tropical waters and has a surface circulation organized and defined in a counterclockwise direction. A cyclone is classified, according to the intensity of its winds, as a tropical

disturbance (light ground-level winds), tropical depression (maximum ground-level winds of 38 miles per hour [61 km/h]), tropical storm (maximum winds in the range of 39 to 73 miles per hour [62 to 112 km/h]), or hurricane (maximum ground-level winds exceeding 74 miles per hour [119 km/h]).

Troposphere

The layer of the atmosphere closest to the ground, its name means "changing sphere," and this layer is where most changes in weather take place. This is also where most of the phenomena of interest in meteorology occur.

Turbulence

Disorderly motion of air composed of small whirlwinds that move within air currents. Atmospheric turbulence is produced by air in a state of continuous change. It can be caused by thermal or convective currents, by differences in terrain and in the velocity of the wind, by conditions along a frontal zone, or by a change in temperature and pressure.

Weather

The state of the atmosphere at a given moment, as it relates to its effects on human activity. This process involves short-term changes in the atmosphere in contrast to the great climatic changes that imply more long-term changes. The terms used to define weather include cloudiness, humidity, precipitation, temperature, visibility, and wind.

Windward

The direction from which the wind is blowing.

Index

A

absorption, 11
acid rain, 86-87
   gas emissions, 86
   gas mixtures, 86
   ozone layer, weakening, 88-89
   pH, 87
   photochemical reaction, 87
   plant consequences, 86
   soil consequences, 87
   vulnerable regions, 87
   water consequences, 87
advection fog, 45
aerosonde pilotless weather aircraft, 71
Africa
   global warming, 91
   potable water, 21
agriculture
   acid rain, 87
   drought, 51
   flooding, 48
   gods and rituals, 76, 77
   monsoons, 30
   tornadoes, 53
air
   atmosphere, 10-11
   circulation changes, 12-13
   collision, 14-15
   currents, 13
   displacement, 12
   weather forecast, 70
aircraft, weather, 71, 81
albedo, solar radiation, 8, 9
almanac, weather forecasting, 65
altocumulus cloud, 39
altostratus cloud, 39
anabatic wind, 26
Andes Mountains, 24-25
anemometer, 67
aneroid barometer, 66
animal
   acid rain, 86, 87
   coral, 82, 83
   ozone layer thinning, 89
   weather folklore, 64, 65
Antarctica, 80, 81, 85
anticyclone, 12, 13, 51, 68
Arctic, 84-85
argon, 10
ash (volcanic), 9
ash tree, weather folklore, 65
Asia
   El Niño, 33, 35
   global warming, 91
   monsoons, 28-29, 30-31
   potable water, 21
atmosphere, 8
   climate change, 90
   cooling, 9
   disturbances, 14
   dynamics, 12-13
   global warming, 83
   layers, 10-11
   paleoclimatology, 80-81
   See also ozone layer
atmospheric pressure, 66
aurora, 10, 16-17
Australia
   drought, 50
   potable water, 21
autonomous underwater vehicle, 70

B

barograph, 66
barometer, 66
biosphere, 8

C

calcareous soil, 87
carbon dioxide (CO_2), 10
   emissions, 82, 83, 86
   increases, 84, 90
   See also greenhouse gas
CFC gas (chlorofluorocarbon gas), 88
chaparral, 25
Chinook wind, 26
cirrocumulus cloud, 39
cirrostratus cloud, 38
cirrus cloud, 38, 39
city, heat islands, 27
climate
   Köppen classification, 79
   temperature and rain, 78
   types, 78-79
climate change, 74-75, 90-91
   causes and effects, 91
   human activity, 81, 82, 90
climate zone, 78-79
   desert, 78
   forest and lakes, 79
   polar mountainous climate, 79
   rainforest, 78
   tundra and taiga, 79
climatic system, 6-7, 8-9
cloud, 38-39
   electrical storms, 46-47
   formation, 12, 14, 20, 38-39
   hurricanes, 56
   interior, 39
   lightning inside, 46
   rain formation, 40-41
   types, 11, 38, 39
   weather folklore, 65
cloud street, 39
coastal breeze, 26, 27
cold climatic zone, 79
cold front, 14, 68
collision (air), 14-15
condensation, 7, 14, 20, 24
   nuclei, 40
   precipitation, 8
continentality effect, 27
convection, 7, 38
convergence, 13, 38
cooling (atmosphere), 9

coral, 82, 83
Coriolis effect, 12, 14, 22
cosmic ray, 11
cryosphere, 8, 9
crystal, water
    formation, 42
    snow, 42-43
    types, 42, 43
cumulonimbus cloud, 38, 52
cumulus cloud, 14, 38
current
    air flow, 13
    cyclonic, 50
    formation, 22-23
    geostrophic balance, 22
    gulf stream, 85
    jet stream, 12, 13, 14
    Labrador, 85
    lake, 23
    ocean: *See* **ocean current**
    subpolar arctic circulating system, 23
    wind influence, 22
cyclone, 5, 12, 13, 28, 36, 57
cyclonic current, 50
cyclonic zone, 12-13

D

data recorder (weather prediction), 67
deep ocean current, 22-23
deforestation, 82, 91
depression, 13, 58, 68
desert, 50, 78
desertification, 5, 50, 82, 83
dew, 42, 44, 65
dew point, 24, 43
dike, 48, 58
divergence, 13
donkey, weather folklore, 64
droplet, formation, 20
drought, 50-51
    global warming, 82

    water runoff, 21
dry-bulb thermometer, 67
dry climatic zone, 78
Dust Bowl, droughts, 50

E

Earth
    climate change, 90-91
    climatic zones, 78-79
    equilibrium, 8-9
    global warming, 82-85
    ocean currents, 22-23
    paleoclimatology, 80-81
    rotation, 12
    satellite image, 6-7
    temperature, 82, 90-91
ecosystem
    destruction, 82
    foundations, 8
Ekman spiral, ocean currents, 22
El Niño, 32-33
    conditions during, 32
    drought, 32-33
    effects, 19, 34-35
    flooding, 34-35
electrical storm, 46-47
    tornadoes, 52
embankment, 48
environment, components, 6
Equator, atmospheric dynamics, 12
erosion, 21
Europe
    global warming, 91
    potable water, 21
evaporation, 7, 8, 20
evaporimeter, 66
exosphere, 10, 16

F

Ferrel cell, 12-13
field capacity, soil, 50
flood control, 48
flood plain, 48
flooding, 48-49
    causes, 48
    dikes, 48, 58
    El Niño, 34-35
    embankment, 48
    global warming, 82, 85
    Hurricane Katrina, 58
    land, 48-49
    monsoons, 30-31
    zones, 85
fog, 44-45
    formation, 44
    radiation, 45
    types, 45
    visibility, 44
folklore, weather: *See* **weather folklore**
forecast: *See* **weather forecast**
fossil fuel
    global warming, 91
    greenhouse effect, 82
freshwater, 21, 74
front, 38
    cold, 14, 68
    occluded, 15, 68
    size, 15
    stationary, 15
    warm, 14, 15, 68
    weather map symbol, 14, 68
frontal fog, 45
frost, 43
Fujita-Pearson scale, 53, 54

G

gas
CFC, 88
density, 10
greenhouse, 8, 9, 84, 90
measurement in paleoclimatology, 80
geopotential weather map, 69
GEOS (Geostationary Operational Environmental Satellite), 72-73
geostrophic balance, 22
glacier
accelerated melting, 74-75, 84-85
Alaska, 74-75
global equilibrium, 8-9
Global Positioning System (GPS), 70
global warming, 82-83
accelerated melting, 84-85
advancing vegetation, 85
Antarctica, 85
cause, 82
climate changes, 5, 82
effects, 82-83
human activity, 82, 84
predictions, 83
rising ocean levels, 5, 82-83, 85
gravity, water circulation, 9
Great Barrier Reef, 83
greenhouse effect, 9, 10, 82-83, 91
greenhouse gas, 8, 9, 81, 82, 84, 90
Greenland, 81, 84
ground-level weather map, 68
gulf stream, 84-85

H

Hadley cell, atmospheric dynamics, 12, 13
hail, 14, 40, 43
Halley, Edmund, 68
heat, greenhouse gas, 8
heat island, 27

heliophanograph, 66
high pressure, 12
See also anticyclone
high pressure ridge, 69
hoar frost, 43
human activity
climate change, 81, 82, 90
pollution, 10, 24, 90
humidity, measuring instruments, 67
hurricane, 34-35, 56-57
damages, 5, 36, 58-59
danger zone, 57
eye and eye wall, 56
formation, 56, 57
hurricane hunter P3 airplane, 71
preparation, 37, 60-61
rotation, 56
safety measures, 60-61
Saffir-Simpson category, 57
tracking, 37
wave height, 57
wind activity, 57
Hurricane Elena, satellite image, 36-37
Hurricane Georges, 4
hurricane hunter P3 airplane, 71
Hurricane Katrina, 58-59
Hurricane Rita, satellite image, 62-63
hydroelectric plant, 49
hydrologic cycle, 20-21
hydrometeor, 42
hydrosphere, 8, 21
hygrothermograph, 67

I-K

ice, 9
polar, 5, 10, 84-85, 90
ice core, paleoclimatology, 80, 81
Intertropical Convergence Zone (ITCZ), 12, 28
inversion fog, 45
isobar, 13, 68
isotherm, 69

jet-stream current, 12, 13
Rossby wave, 14
katabatic wind, 26
Köppen climate classification, 79

L

La Niña
conditions during, 33
effects, 32, 35
Labrador current, 85
lake, seasonal water circulation, 23
land
temperature distribution, 26-27, 29
weather data, 70
lenticular cloud, 39
lightning, 46-47
electrical potential, 47
origin, 46
types, 46
lightning rod, 47
lithosphere, 8, 9
Lorenz, Edward, 5
low pressure, 12, 13, 46, 56, 68
See also cyclone
low pressure trough, 69

M

magnetosphere, 16, 17
map, weather: *See* weather map
maritime sounding probe, 71
maximum thermometer, 67
mercury barometer, 66
mesosphere, 11
meteor, 11
meteorological aircraft, 71, 81
meteorological buoy, 71
meteorological shelter, 67

meteorological station, 67, 70
meteorology, 62-73
methane, concentration, 80-81, 90
minimum thermometer, 67
mist, 44, 45
monsoon, 19, 28-29, 30-31
    areas affected, 28
    effects, 30-31
    formation in India, 28-29, 31
    intertropical influence, 28
    North America, 28
Moon, weather folklore, 65
mountain, 24-25
    Andes, 24-25
    barrier to wind and moisture, 9
    climatic effects, 24-25
    climatic zones, 79
    descending wind, 25
    high, 11
    major ranges, 25
    monsoons, 29
    uneven mountainside, 25
    vegetation, 25
    winds, 26
mythology and religion, 76-77
    Aztecs, 77
    Egyptians, 76
    Greeks, 76
    Hindus, 77
    Incas, 77
    Japanese, 77
    Mayans, 77
    Orient, 77
    pre-Columbians, 77
    Romans, 76-77

N

nimbostratus cloud, 39
nitrogen, 10, 17
noctilucent cloud, 11
North America

El Niño, 35
    global warming, 90
    monsoons, 28
    potable water, 21
    tornadoes, 53, 54-55
Northern Hemisphere, 22, 28, 52, 56

O

oak tree, weather folklore, 64-65
occluded front, 15, 68
ocean
    circulation, 9
    current: *See* **ocean current**
    El Niño, 32-33, 34-35
    hurricanes, 56
    level changes, 5, 32, 83. 85
    temperature distribution, 26-27, 29
    water return, 20
    weather data, 70
ocean current, 22-23
    changes, 84
    deep, 22, 23
    formation, 22-23
    gulf stream, 85
    Labrador, 85
    surface, 22
oceanographic ship, 70
oxygen, 10, 17, 88
ozone, 10, 11, 83, 88, 89
ozone layer, 88-89
    atmosphere, 11
    CFC gas, 88
    deterioration, 88
    global warming, 83
    thinning, 90
    weakening, 88-89

P

paleoclimatology, 80-81

    chronology, 80-81
    gas measurement, 80
    human activity, 81
    methane concentration, 81
    samples, 80, 81
permafrost, 9
perspiration, 20
pH, acid rain, 87
photochemical reaction, 87
photosynthesis, 9, 82
pinecone, weather folklore, 64
plant
    acid rain, 86
    flooding, 48
    hydrologic cycle, 20
    ozone layer, 89
    weather folklore, 64, 65
polar cell, 13
polar ice
    cap, 10
    melting, 5, 84-85, 90
polar mountainous climate, 79
pollution, 11, 24
    See also **acid rain**
precipitation
    condensation, 8
    droplet formation, 20
    formation, 14, 21, 24, 40-43
    rain: *See* **rain**
    sleet, 42
    snow, 14, 25, 40, 42-43
    snowfall record, 42
pressure
    high, 12, 69
    low, 12, 13, 68
psychrometer, 67

radar station, 71
radiation
    solar, 8, 9, 11, 16

ultraviolet, 7, 88, 89
radiation fog, 45
radiosonde, 70, 71
rain, 18, 78
  acid, 87
  causes, 14, 25
  climatic zones, 78
  flooding, 48
  formation, 40-41
  global warming, 82
  importance, 18-19
  measuring instruments, 67
  monsoons, 19, 28-29
  torrential, 19, 49
  toxic, 86-87
  typhoons, 19
rain gauge, 67
rain meter, 67
rainforest, 78
religion: *See* **mythology and religion**
rocket probe, 10
Rossby wave, 14
rotation, Earth, 12

S

safety, hurricanes, 60-61
Saffir-Simpson category, hurricanes, 56
salt water (sea water), 21, 90
satellite, 72-73
  geostationary, 72
  infrared images, 71
  meteorology, 10, 37, 62-63, 70, 71
  military, 10
  mobile, 72-73
  polar orbit, 72
season, lake circulation variations, 23
seaweed, weather folklore, 64
shooting star, 11
silicate soil, 87
skin cancer, ozone layer weakening, 89
sky, colors, 16-17

sleet, 42
snail, weather folklore, 65
snow, 14, 25, 40, 42-43
snowfall, record annual, 42
soil
  acid rain consequences, 87
  calcareous, 87
  drought, 50
  field capacity, 51
  flooding effects, 48
  saturated, 50
  silicate, 87
  water, proportion of, 51
  wilting, 51
solar radiation, 8, 9, 16
  absorption, 11
  reflection, 11
solar wind, 16, 17
sounding probe, launchable, 71
South America
  El Niño, 32-33, 35
  global warming, 90
  potable water, 21
Southern Hemisphere, 22, 28, 52, 56
stationary front, 15, 68
stratocumulus cloud, 39
stratosphere, 11
stratus cloud, 38, 39
subpolar arctic current, 23
Sun, 9
  cosmic ray, 11
  radiation, 8-9
  sunlight measurement, 66
  ultraviolet ray, 10-11
  volcanic eruption, 9
surface ocean current, 22
swallow (bird), weather folklore, 64

T

taiga, 25, 79
temperate zone, 78

temperature
  atmospheric dynamics, 12
  climate zones, 78
  differences over land and ocean, 26-27, 29
  earth, over the years, 82, 90
  global warming, 82-83
  greenhouse effect, 10
  measuring instruments, 67
  variation, 7
thermal expansion, 84
thermal inversion, 11
thermometer, types, 67
thermosphere, 10
thunder, 46
tide, 22
toad, weather folklore, 64
topography, irregularities, 12
tornado, 52-53
  causes, 52
  damages, 5, 52, 54-55
  formation, 52
  Fujita-Pearson scale, 53, 54
  ten most devastating, 55
  United States, 54-55
  where and when, 53
  wind velocity, 53
toxic rain: *See* **acid rain**
trade winds, 12, 32
transpiration, 20
Tri-State tornado (United States), 54-55
tropical cyclone, 36-37
  See also **cyclone; hurricane; typhoon**
tropical depression, 58
tropical zone, 78
troposphere, 11, 38
tundra, 25, 79
typhoon, 19, 36, 57

U-V

ultraviolet radiation (UV radiation), 88, 89
  CFC gas, 88

ozone, 7, 90
types, 89
ultraviolet ray, 10-11
valley, wind, 26
velocity, wind
minimum/maximum, 13
tornado, 52
visibility, fog, 44
volcanic eruption, 9

W

warm front, 14, 15, 68
water, 7, 20-21
accumulation, 48-49
acid rain consequences, 87
availability, 21
circulation, 9
clouds, 39
distribution worldwide, 21
droplet formation, 20
dry zones, 50
evaporation measurement, 66
gods and rituals, 76-77
gaseous state, 20
liquid state, 21
ocean currents, 22-23
return to ocean, 20
runoff, 21
scarcity, 50-51
seasonal lake circulation, 23
soil saturation, 50
solid state, 21
types, 20, 21
underground circulation, 20-21
water cycle, 20-21
water vapor, 10, 20
weather aircraft, 71, 81
weather folklore, 64-65
almanac forecast, 65
clear sunset, 65
clouds, 65

Moon, 65
morning dew, 65
signs from plants and animals, 64, 65
weather prediction, 65
wind, 65
weather forecast, 70-71
acoustic signal, 70
aerosonde pilotless weather aircraft, 71
air, 70
almanacs, 65
artificial satellites, 71, 72-73
autonomous underwater vehicle, 70
better forecasts, 71
data collection, 70
factors affecting, 5
hurricane hunter P3 airplane, 71
land, 70
launchable sounding probe, 71
maritime sounding probe, 71
meteorological aircraft, 71, 81
meteorological buoy, 71
meteorological centers, 71
meteorological station, 70
oceanographic ship, 70
radar station, 71
radiosonde, 70, 71
sea, 70
sources, 70
weather map, 68-69
cold front, 14, 68
history of, 68
isobar, 68
nomenclature, 68
overcast sky, 69
symbols, 68
upper-air, 69
upper-level, 69
warm front, 14, 68
wind velocity, 69
winds, 69
weather prediction, 4-5
anemometer, 67
artificial satellites, 72-73
barograph, 66
barometers, 66

data recorder, 67
evaporimeter, 66
heliophanograph, 66
hygrothermograph, 67
information compilation, 66-67
meteorological shelter, 67
psychrometer, 67
rain gauge, 67
rain meter, 67
thermometers, 67
weather folklore, 64-65
weather maps, 68-69
weather stations, 67
weather vane, 67
workplace, 66-67
weather station, 67
weather systems analysis, 13
weather vane, 67
wet-bulb thermometer, 67
whirlwind, 26
wilting, water scarcity, 51
wind, 7, 8
coastal breeze, 26, 27
cold fronts, 14
continentality effect, 27
direction, 13
hurricane, 57
measuring instruments, 67
monsoon: *See* **monsoon**
mountains, 24-25, 26
ocean currents, 22
solar: *See* **solar wind**
tides, 22
tornado: *See* **tornado**
trade, 12, 32
types, 26
valleys, 26
velocity, 13, 69
weather maps, 69
whirlwind, 26
World Meteorological Organization, 70